Essential
Prague

by
CHRISTOPHER AND MELANIE RICE

Christopher Rice is a writer specialising in East European affairs, and holds a PhD from the Centre for Russian and East European Studies at Birmingham University. His wife, Melanie, is also a writer and they have worked together on several children's books and guides.

Produced by AA Publishing

Written by Christopher and Melanie Rice
Peace and Quiet section
by Paul Sterry
Series Adviser: Ingrid Morgan
Series Controller: Nia Williams
Copy editor: Jo Sturges

Edited, designed and produced by AA Publishing. Maps ©
The Automobile Association 1992

Distributed in the United Kingdom by the Publishing Division of The Automobile Association, Fanum House, Basingstoke, Hampshire, RG21 2EA.

The contents of this publication are believed correct at the time of printing. Nevertheless, the publishers cannot accept responsibility for errors or omissions, nor for changes in details given. We have tried to ensure accuracy in this guide, but things do change and we would be grateful if readers could advise us of any inaccuracies they may encounter.

A CIP catalogue record for this book is available from the British Library.

ISBN 0 7495 0315 7

Published by The Automobile Association

Typesetting: Tradespools Ltd, Frome, Somerset

Colour separation: Mullis Morgan Ltd, London

Printed in Italy by Printers SRL, Trento

Front cover picture: St Nicholas's Church

This book employs a
simple rating system to
help choose which
places to visit.

 do not miss

 see if you can

 worth seeing if
you have time

INTRODUCTION

The French poet Guillaume Apollinaire wrote of Prague as 'a golden ship sailing majestically on the Vltava'. No European city, with the possible exception of Venice, wears superlatives more graciously and easily than this dazzling jewel, set among the mellow Bohemian woodlands, beside the drowsy banks of the meandering River Vltava. Prague has grown, over a period of a thousand years, into a breathtaking architectural monument, a miraculous synthesis of architectural styles. But this 'city of a hundred spires' is much more than a cultural treasure house. Prague today is a thrusting commercial and administrative centre, home to more than 1,300,000 people and the capital of one of the most important countries of Central Europe.

A Peaceful Revolution

It took the Czech people just three weeks, in November and December 1989, to rid themselves of forty years of Communist tyranny, in what has become known as The Velvet Revolution. The hero of the hour (and a hero still) was Václav Havel, playwright, dissident and signatory of Charter 77. On 1 January 1990, to popular acclaim, Havel was inaugurated as President of the newborn republic after a parliamentary vote in the historical Václav Chamber of Prague Castle, where the Bohemian kings had once been crowned. He was invested in this high office by Alexander Dubček, instigator of the liberalising movement in the spring of 1968—known as 'Prague Spring', and now chairman of the Federal Assembly. With typical modesty, Havel chose to continue living in his old apartment on what is now the Rašínovo Embankment overlooking the Vltava. His office, however, is in the Castle.

In June 1990 the Czechs went to the polls in the first free elections since 1946. Twenty-two parties competed for the votes of 11 million Czechs and Slovaks, not all seriously – a 'Friends of Beer' Party, for example, proposed an annual ale festival in Plseň! The winners were Civic Forum and its Slovak sister party, Public Against Violence. Utterly discredited were the Communists, whose symbol of two cherries was mercilessly satirised by the other parties (one poster portrayed Stalin wearing a pair of cherry earrings).

Since then, the Czechs have been determined to eradicate every vestige of their Communist past. The names of Marx, Engels, Lenin and the first Soviet-backed president, Klement Gottwald, have been removed from streets and metro stations and replaced by more suitable, home-spun heroes like Tomáš Masaryk, founder of Czechoslovakia, and Jan Palach, one of the martyrs of 1968.

As Soviet troops began pulling out from military bases like Milovice, hundreds of prominent dissidents and former exiles began returning to their native land: among them the theatre director, Jan Grossman, the film director, Jan Nemec who made his name in the 1960s, and the novelist, Milan Kundera, author of *The Unbearable Lightness of Being*, now a major film.

Waking up to a Hangover

By the time US President George Bush arrived in Prague to join the celebrations of the first anniversary of the revolution, the Czechs had come down to earth with a bump. Substantial, across-the-board price rises were in the offing. Petrol rationing was being introduced, as the government prepared for the first time to pay the Soviet Union in precious hard currency. Pessimistic forecasters were predicting a rise in

INTRODUCTION

Elegant façades in pastel colours surround Old Town Square

unemployment beyond one million in a workforce of 7.5 million. Hard-pressed industrialists were trying to come to terms with the removal of public subsidies from the newly privatised industries. Pollution, rising crime, tensions between Czechs and Slovaks and the decline in public services were other issues on people's minds in the winter of 1990–91. The climate of political uncertainty affected the government itself, as a tug-of-war developed within Civic Forum between the old dissident Left and new, Right-of-centre politicians like the finance minister, Václav Klaus.

Despite the gloomy prognostications, the Czechs are quietly determined to see things through to a better future. And to the casual observer at least, Prague is as cheerful and radiant as ever. These are exciting times. In 1992 the International Mozart Foundation will launch a Mozart Academy and sponsor a feast of operas by the great composer in what will be a newly-restored Týl Theatre. This is the kind of thing that is encouraging tourists from all over Europe to flock to Prague.

A City for all Seasons

There is so much to see and do in Prague that, no matter how long your stay, you will be spoilt for choice. First there are the sights, dominated by the magnificent Prague Castle and the palaces of Hradčany. Then, clinging to the hillside, the baroque splendours of the Malá Strana, crowned by Dietzenhofer's masterpiece, the Church of St Nicholas. Across the river is the former Jewish Ghetto of Josefov with its 13th-century synagogue (still functioning) and a medieval cemetery crammed with 12,000 tombstones. The highlight of the Staré Město is Old Town Square with its eccentric clock tower, Gothic and baroque churches and former palaces, decked out in pastel pink, grey, cream and yellow. Finally, there is the New Town (in Prague this means 14th-century!) at the centre of which is world-famous Wenceslas Square with its flower-strewn shrine to the martyrs of the revolution, its shops and hotels, restaurants and wine bars, cafés and nightclubs.

Prague has a cultural tradition going back centuries. Hadyn, Beethoven and Liszt all walked these streets and Mozart was a regular visitor to Prague, conducting in the Týl Theatre. It was here that *Figaro* was first acclaimed and *Don Giovanni* received its first performance. Mozart stayed at the Villa Bertramka, where there is now a museum in his honour. Of the home-grown talent one need only mention Dvořák, Smetana, Janaček and Martinů, whose works can regularly be heard in the National Theatre or the Dvořák Concert Hall. You can go to see a play (in Czech) at the Na zăbradlí, the Nová scéna or the Vinohrady theatres. Prague is famous for its puppet shows, mime and the spectacular Magic Lantern, an experience not to be missed. If you are still in a literary frame of mind, you can visit any number of Kafka's houses, the most famous of which is in Golden Lane, in the grounds of Prague Castle, or pay a visit to U kalicha (the Chalice), pub haunt of Hašek's *Good Soldier Švejk*. Prague is famous for these beery, smoke-filled taverns, or *pivnice*, dispensing some of the finest lagers in Europe. These medieval taverns have traditionally brewed their own beer and many still do. They often have their own loyal customers who prefer one brew to another. Often there is entertainment in the taverns, especially satire and avant-garde comedy.

Equally good value are the eating houses of Prague, though you won't find it easy to get a table. Leave plenty of room for a plate full of pork cutlets and dumplings, served in a rich brown sauce and washed down with a fine bottle of Moravian red wine. If you've got room for a strudel, so much the better. If you want to prolong the evening, Prague's jazz clubs, discotheques and late night bars will carry you well into the small hours – Wenceslas Square is the area to head for.

Prague is a city to stroll in (there are parks and gardens galore, especially on the left bank of the river), but tired feet will find solace in the excellent public transport system which includes a super-efficient metro. No-one becomes bored with Prague but if you want an excursion, there is no shortage of options: a boat trip on the Vltava, a visit to Charles IV's castle at Karlštejn, a leisurely day out in the spa town of Karlovy Vary – or just a visit to the zoo.

A Friendly Welcome

Everywhere you go in the city you find the people friendly, courteous and helpful. They are also outgoing and self-confident, as you will soon be aware if you meet them in the relaxed surroundings of pub or restaurant. Try to engage them in conversation (even if you don't know Czech) and you will be surprised at how many will produce at least a smattering of English, now that Russian has been replaced as the compulsory foreign language at schools and colleges. You never know – you may end up exchanging addresses and forming friendships which will bring you back to Prague for many years to come.

The city which outshone the stars has lost none of its splendour

BACKGROUND

One City, Many Towns

According to legend, Prague was founded sometime in the 9th century after Libuše, a princess belonging to the Čech tribe, had climbed the hilltop now known as Vyšehrad, and looked upon a visionary city whose splendour outreached the stars. She took as her consort the ploughman Přemysl, who realised her dream and established the line of rulers known as the Přemyslid dynasty. A thousand years later, the composer Bedřich Smetana, used the legend as the basis for his 'festive tableau', *Libuše*, written for the opening of the Czech National Theatre. Smetana had already immortalised Vyšehrad in his symphonic cycle, *Ma Vlast*. The castle here once vied in importance with Pražsky Hrad (Prague Castle) but was later allowed to fall into neglect. The castle and the settlement of Hradčany, on the opposite bank of the Vltava, was founded by the first Přemyslid ruler, Duke Bořivoj, in the 9th century. His grandson Václav (Wenceslas) became Duke of Bohemia and he built a church dedicated to St Vitus within the castle compound before he was murdered in

BACKGROUND

The murder of Wenceslas by his brother, Boleslav. The ruling elite did not like the fact that Wenceslas was a devout Christian; the treaty he made with Germany was the last straw

about 929 by his own brother. Wenceslas was later canonised and became the patron saint of Czechoslovakia. This is the 'Good King' Wenceslas of the 19th-century English carol, though the narrative is a complete invention with no basis in Czech literature.

The earliest Prague Castle was a timber structure, surrounded by a ditch and moat, but in 1135 Prince Soběslav I began a major programme of reconstruction which was continued by his successors well into the 13th century. The completed Romanesque fortress comprised newly-fortified walls and watch towers, a remodelled cathedral of St Vitus, the convent and basilica of St George, a bishop's residence and a royal palace.

In 1157 the wooden bridge spanning the Vltava was destroyed by flooding. It was replaced almost immediately by a new stone bridge, named after Judith, wife of Duke Vladislav who became the first king of Bohemia. By then, the settlement on the opposite bank of the river, known as Staré Město – the Old Town, was well entrenched as a thriving centre of international trade and commerce and Prague established its place as the leading city of Bohemia. Archaeological evidence suggests that the entire area from Celetná to the river was heavily built up and densely populated. Only the large Jewish community was excluded and confined behind the walls of a ghetto in the quarter known today as Josefov. The entire town was enclosed within fortifications, begun in about 1230, which followed the route now taken by Národní, Na přikopě (At the Moat) and Revoluční streets.

In 1257 King Ottokar II founded a third settlement, the 'New Town Below Prague Castle', now known as the Malá Strana or Lesser Quarter. Growth centred on the square called Malostranské náměstí, originally the outer earthworks of Prague Castle. Markets, shops and houses occupied by millers, brewers, lawyers, physicians and wealthy burghers were developed here and a Town Hall was built near the first St Nicholas Church (1283). The Augustinian monastery of St Thomas on Letenská dates from the same period, but the most impressive religious foundation was undoubtedly the fortified monastery of Maltese knights. The Church authorities exercised independent administration over the entire area, which included more than 50 merchants' houses. The Carmelite convent and church of St Mary Magdalene, on modern Karmelitská, dates from the early 14th century.

No monarch had a greater influence on the development of medieval Prague than Charles IV, King of Bohemia from 1346 and subsequently Holy Roman Emperor. One of the best educated figures of the period, Charles had studied at the famed University of Paris and was determined to put Prague on the intellectual map. A new university, the first in the region, received its charter in 1348 and attracted scholars from all over the Empire, including distinguished Humanists like Cola di Rienzi and the Bohemian Chancellor, Johann of Neumark. The university moved to its present home, the Carolinum, in 1356. A great deal of building work took place in the Old Town during Charles' reign, including the redevelopment of the Týn church and the construction of a new bridge across the Vltava which now bears Charles' name.

Development outside the Old Town was even more remarkable. On Hradčany, the Emperor commissioned, first, Matthias of Arras and, later, the renowned Peter Parler to rebuild the cathedral of St Vitus in the fashionable Gothic style. The settlement around the castle grew apace, extending as far as Loretánská, where Parler had his own house (now the Hrzán Palace) and the area of Petřín Hill called Nový Svět (New World). Here also Charles built a new system of fortifications marking the boundary of the Lesser Quarter, including the 'Hunger Wall', a public works project conceived to give assistance to the hungry and unemployed of the city. Part of the wall still stands today.

With the building of a fourth settlement, Nové Město (New Town), Prague became one of the largest urban communities in medieval Europe. The New Town is also remarkable for being a planned development where the width of streets, the heights of houses and the materials to be used were all strictly pre-ordained. At the heart was a wide street called the horse market, known today as Wenceslas Square.

Catholics, Protestants and Reformers

Charles IV's death in 1378 coincided with the onset of the Great Schism when three Popes vied for control over Christendom. The resulting scandal only served to exacerbate tensions between clergy and laity which had long been smouldering beneath the surface. The reformist teachings of the English theologian John Wycliffe were brought to Prague with the active encouragement of Charles' daughter, Anne of Bohemia, who had married King Richard II of England in 1382. Wycliffe's views were also supported in part by Jan Hus, a professor at Prague University and, from 1402, a renowned preacher at the newly-founded Bethlehem Chapel. It was in the austere setting of this barn-like building, designed to contrast with the Gothic excesses of the surrounding churches, that Hus called for a return to basic Christian precepts and values, for the redistribution of the church's secular wealth and for greater weight to be placed on the authority of the scriptures. Nationalist tensions between Czechs and Germans at the university added fuel to the

Jan Hus being burned at the stake. An outspoken critic of the established Church, Hus was supported by many of the people. His death marked the beginning of more than 20 years of war

developing crisis, which rapidly spun out of control under the feeble rule of Wenceslas IV. The selling of indulgences (a form of pardon for sins that had been commited) provoked ever fiercer denunciations from Hus and his supporters and led ultimately to his excommunication. In 1415, having received a safe conduct from the Emperor Sigismund, Hus and a group of companions set out for the Swiss city of Constance where a Council of the Church had promised him a hearing. It was a trap – he was immediately arrested, summarily tried and on 6 July burnt at the stake.

In Bohemia this act of treachery provoked a situation bordering on civil war. In 1419 one of Hus's champions, a fellow-preacher named Jan Zelivsky, led the poorer inhabitants of the New Town in an attack on the Town Hall, during which a number of councillors were hurled from the chamber windows in an incident which later became known as the First Defenestration of Prague.

The next provocation came from the Church. In 1420 Pope Martin V proclaimed a crusade against the heretics, a call which was widely and bloodily taken up. The Hussites, under their one-eyed general, the resourceful Jan Žižka, assembled their forces east of Prague, where they successfully overcame Sigismund's army at the battle of Vítkov (now the suburb of Žižkov). In the general confusion which preceded the battle, much of the Malá Strana was destroyed. The war dragged on for the next twenty years, with the Imperial side repeatedly offering tactical concessions which were subsequently withdrawn. When George of Poděbrady assumed the throne in 1458, he supported the reformers and an uneasy truce prevailed.

The period of dynastic conflict which followed George's death in 1471 led ultimately to the accession of Ferdinand I, brother of the German Emperor, and 400 years of Habsburg rule ensued.

The Second Defenestration of Prague, in 1618. Three courtiers were thrown from a window of Prague Castle; 30 years of appalling war followed

Germans, Jesuits and the Thirty Years War

Ferdinand lost no time in establishing a presence in the Bohemian capital. He invited the most imaginative Italian designers and architects of the day to build the summer palace in the gardens immediately north of the walls of Prague Castle. The palace is known as the Belvedere and was for his wife Anna. Much more significant, however, was his decision in 1556 to invite the Jesuits, shock troops of the Counter-Reformation, to begin proselytising among the heretical inhabitants of the city. Over the next century and a half they acquired vast amounts of property in the Old Town, much of which was demolished to make way for the grim, fortress-like Clementinum, conceived as an intellectual and moral bastion of Catholicism. Religious conflict was always at the root of the Empire's problems and nowhere more so than in Bohemia. In May 1618, incensed by the behaviour of the Emperor's Catholic officials, representatives of the Protestant nobility led a march on Hradčany, in the course of which three prominent courtiers were pushed from a window in the castle (the Second Defenestration of Prague). This seemingly innocuous incident ushered in one of the most brutal periods of modern European history, the Thirty Years War. Bohemia was ravaged and Prague saw some of the worst excesses. In 1620 the Emperor's Catholic forces routed his opponents at the battle of the White Mountain, now the Prague suburb of Břevnov. The Imperial troops were let loose on the city and wholesale executions followed. Among those singled out for special punishment were the 27 Protestant noblemen adjudged to have been leaders of the revolt, who were publicly executed in Old Town Square.

By the end of the war in 1648 the Habsburgs were back in the saddle. Austrian rule was repressive and Bohemia was reduced to the status of provincial backwater. Power was exercised from Vienna, the estates of Protestant noblemen were confiscated and redistributed among foreigners, and the indigenous culture was suppressed by a policy of Germanisation. In Prague the final triumph of Catholicism was domination by the Jesuits. Work on the

Clementinum continued throughout the 17th and 18th centuries. But their greatest imprint was made on the Lesser Quarter. The Jesuits had already acquired the medieval church of St Nicholas in 1625. Fifty years later a vast site in the middle of the square was cleared in order to make way for a school and college. Finally, in the early decades of the 18th century, the old church itself was demolished and replaced by the magnificent, late baroque monument which still stands sentinel over the district today. By this time, however, the Jesuits' days were numbered. The Enlightenment brought with it the notion of religious tolerance and, in 1773, that most intolerant of orders was abolished and their property confiscated.

Prague in the Baroque Era

If Habsburg rule was a severe blow to the nationalist aspirations of the Czech people, it was by no means an unmitigated disaster, especially for Prague, which was refashioned as a baroque jewel in the Austrian crown. Italian, German and indigenous artists all made distinctive contributions. The great Bavarian architects Christoph and Kilian Dientzenhofer were responsible for dozens of projects besides playing a role in the development of the Clementinum, the Loreto and the reconstruction of Prague Castle. Giovanni Alliprandi designed the Hartig and Kaiserstein Palaces in the Lesser Quarter and the Sternberg Palace on Hradčany, while František Kaňka was responsible for the Černin Palace on Petřín Hill, as well as for parts of the Clementinum and the design of the Vrtba Terraces on Karmelitská. Sculptors too made their mark. Ferdinand Brockoff and Bernhardt Braun contributed many of the most effective statues on the Charles Bridge, while Johann Bendl added sculptures to the façade of the church of St Salvator in Křižovnické náměstí. Building on such a colossal scale made exceptional demands on the inventiveness of artists. Among those rising to the challenge were Karel Skréta, F Q Voget, V V Reiner and J L Kracker, whose paintings adorn the walls and ceilings of the most sumptuous of Prague's baroque churches. Some of Skréta's best work is in the gallery of St George's Convent.

The Hotel Evropa, in Wenceslas Square. It was built between 1903 and 1935

Habsburg patronage also brought some of the greatest musicians of the century to Prague. Haydn played the organ here and Beethoven visited in 1796, but the city's closest associations are with Mozart, an Austrian whose reception here was much more enthusiastic than in frosty Vienna. During his first visit, in January 1787, he and his wife Constanze stayed with Count Johann Thun at his palace on the slopes of Hradčany (now the British Embassy). The Mozarts returned in October for the premiere of *Don Giovanni*, guests this time of F X Dušek and his wife, Josepha – a noted soprano – at their suburban retreat, the Villa Bertramka. The score was completed here only just in time for the first performance, which took place at the Nostitz (Týl) Theatre later in the month. In the autumn of 1791 Mozart was in Prague again, this time to oversee the production of a new opera, *La Clemenza di Tito*, commissioned by Leopold II for his coronation as King of Bohemia. Already ill and overworked, Mozart hurried back to Vienna, only to die there the following December. Leopold's coronation was an attempt to mollify the Bohemian nobility, who were becoming restive under Habsburg rule. Part of Mozart's popularity in Prague was because his audience there had detected an element of subversion in *The Marriage of Figaro* when it was played here: enough to make him a hero.

The Age of Czech Nationalism

When one considers the sheer extent of German influence in Prague at the turn of the 19th century, such unrest is hardly surprising. In 1815, only one in every three inhabitants was a Czech. Germans dominated the administration, the streets bore German names (Na příkopě became the Graben for example) and German was the language of polite and educated society. All this was to change, as industrialisation created a predominantly Czech working class, whose antagonism towards the Habsburgs was shared by students and liberal intellectuals. Matters came to a head during the revolutions of 1848, when the subject peoples of the Empire made their voices heard for the first time. In June a Slav congress, convening in Prague, brought workers and students on to the streets for an anti-Austrian demonstration which provided General Windischgrätz with the excuse to send in the troops. Habsburg rule was eventually restored but with less conviction than before, allowing the Czechs and the other minorities of the far-flung Empire to raise the status of their language and institutions. A National Theatre was opened in Prague in 1881 and a National Museum in 1893 but little progress if any was made in the direction of political autonomy before World War I.

Entering the Twentieth Century

Austria-Hungary entered the conflict on the side of Germany and the Czechs inevitably became embroiled. In 1915 an exiled philosophy professor, Tomáš Masaryk, called on Czechs and Slovaks to organise against the Central Powers at the same time as thousands of Czech soldiers at the front were deserting to the Russians. A special Czech legion was formed which now began fighting on the Allied side. This was enough for Masaryk to win a commitment from Britain and France to future independence. The promise was honoured and, on 28 October 1918, the Republic of Czechoslovakia was proclaimed in Prague's Municipal Hall, Obecní dům.

The new state was eventually destroyed by the same ethnic tensions that had bedevilled its predecessor. Conflict between Czechs and

Slovaks and between the Czechs and the other national minorities (Germans, Romanians, Hungarians and Poles) was never far from the surface and occasionally erupted into open hostility. The three million Germans of the Sudetenland had hoped to become part of Austria but the Great Powers had decided otherwise. Smouldering resentment flared into outright opposition during the Depression, when unemployment hit the population of this heavily industrialised region very hard. Hitler encouraged the Sudeten Germans to demand ever closer ties with the Reich. The Czechoslovak government under President Beneš offered concessions, while standing firm on matters of principle. But the Czechs' determination to ride out the crisis, even to go to war if necessary, foundered at Munich in September 1938 when France, under pressure from Britain, finally deserted them. The Sudetenland was sacrificed without the Czechs being consulted and, six months later, German troops marched into Prague.

For the Jews the consequences were catastrophic. Ninety per cent of the inhabitants of the Prague ghetto, or more than 60,000 people, perished in concentration camps during World War II – in Terezín (Theresienstadt) alone, more than 15,000 children died. Although the Red Army crossed the Carpathians in October 1944, Prague was the last European capital to be liberated. By a miracle, its priceless architectural heritage survived almost intact, despite hand-to-hand fighting in the cellars and basements of Old Town Square.

After World War II

The Czechoslovak Communist Party rode the tide of pro-Soviet feeling which swept the country after the war, to win nearly 40 per cent of the vote in free elections held in 1946. But in May 1948, following a series of political manoeuvres of dubious legality, the Communists staged a coup. A sham constitution was then introduced by the new President, Klement Gottwald. Beneš resigned in protest and the foreign minister, Jan Masaryk (son of Tomáš), was found dead in the courtyard of Prague's Černin Palace, almost certainly murdered. Using

BACKGROUND

Brief victory. In the autumn of 1968 Soviet tanks rolled into Prague, sent to crush a flowering of freedom. The tanks won but not before some had been destroyed

the familiar Stalinist blueprint, Gottwald and his successors now set about transforming Czechoslovakia into a totalitarian state and loyal satellite of the Soviet Union. Industry was nationalised, agriculture collectivised and repression institutionalised as the Czechs were railroaded into Comecon and the Warsaw Pact. At least Prague was spared the worst excesses of the architectural 'renaissance' visited on most of the other socialist capitals, though there was one blot on the landscape: an 18,000-ton (18,288,000 kg), 150-foot (45 metre) high statue of Stalin, glowering over the city from a perch high above the Letná Gardens. It was dismantled in 1962. By the mid-1960s there were calls from within the Communist Party for an economic and political facelift. In January 1968, the hard-line President, Antonin Novotny, was replaced as Party Leader by the reformer, Alexander Dubček, who introduced the slogan 'Socialism with a human face'. During the heady months of the 'Prague Spring' the Czechs enjoyed a degree of freedom they had not experienced for more than 30 years. But the Soviets were horrified by moves like the abolition of censorship, the rehabilitation of former dissidents, the challenge to economic orthodoxy and the questioning of the leading role of the

Party. Dubček and his supporters successfully fought off the dark threats, dire warnings and backstair intrigues orchestrated by Moscow before finally succumbing to the bludgeon of military force. On 21 August 1968 the tanks rolled into Prague and the reforms, as fragile as the flowers proffered to the bemused drivers, were crushed.

The Velvet Revolution

For the next twenty years, Czechoslovakia was subjected to the 'normalising' policies of a new leader, Gustáv Husák. One-third of all Communists were expelled from the Party, more than a quarter of a million officials lost their jobs, 50,000 Czechs went into exile and thousands of prominent intellectuals, like the writer Milan Kundera, were forced into menial jobs as window cleaners and lift attendants while their works were uniformly banned. Meanwhile, the majority of the population was cynically 'bought off' by a carefully managed consumer boom. It was all too much for some. On 16 January 1969 a 20-year-old philosophy student, Jan Palach, set fire to himself in Wenceslas Square. Six weeks later, his brave but tragic example was followed by Jan Zajic. Others, like the dissident

Memorials to Jan Palach

playwright Václav Havel, took a more considered course, and in 1977 the Charter Movement was founded to monitor the government's activities and its compliance with the Helsinki Accords on human rights.

Seen in retrospect, Mikhail Gorbachev's arrival on the scene in the mid-1980s, armed with the twin policies of *perestroika* and *glasnost*, was bound to cause seismic tremors in the bowels of the old Stalinist empire. But no one could have predicted the tumultuous events of 1989 when all of Eastern Europe threw off its chains as if at a given signal. In Czechoslovakia the period has become known as The Velvet Revolution. It began on 17 November when 15,000 people assembled in Vyšehrad to commemorate the anniversary of the Nazi occupation. The intention was to march to Wenceslas Square but the police blocked the way at Národní, allowing red beret units to charge the peaceful demonstrators with batons. One student, Martin Šmíd, was killed and hundreds more injured. Actors and theatre employees responded by calling a strike and overnight the auditoria became meeting halls, echoing to the sound of political debate. The outcome was the setting up of Civic Forum, which began life in the Drama Club theatre near Wenceslas Square. All Prague was now in ferment. The students joined the strike, candlelit processions wound their way around the centre of the city and public rallies became routine.

One particularly moving moment was when the banned singer Marta Kubišová sang the National Anthem to an ecstatic audience. The re-emergence of the old hero Alexander Dubček was equally memorable. Meanwhile, government and Party figures were manoeuvred into dialogue. On 26 November, while foreign journalists crowded expectantly in the lobby of the Intercontinental Hotel, the leaders of Civic Forum were negotiating with members of the Central Committee in Obecní dům.

Constitutional changes, including the promise of free elections, were wrung from the authorities and the resignations began. Premier Adamec was followed, on 9 December, by Husák himself. With the formation of a new government, a fresh page in Czech history was turned.

WHAT TO SEE

It is a pleasure to be able to say, without exaggeration, that Prague is one of the most beautiful cities in Europe. It is also among the most fascinating. Indeed Goethe called it 'the most exquisite gem in the world's stone crown', and it is often described lyrically as the 'Mother of Cities', or 'The Golden City'. Fortunately Prague is uniquely well preserved, thanks to the happy accident of having avoided major bombing during World War II.

Even to cover the main points of interest you will need three hectic days, but given the

A view over tree-covered slopes to Prague's red rooftops

abundance of unique architectural and historic sites it will quickly become obvious that Prague is best seen at leisure.

For sightseeing purposes Prague divides naturally into its four medieval quarters: **Hradčany** (Castle District); **Malá Strana** (Lesser Town); **Staré Město** (Old Town) and **Nové Město** (New Town). Perhaps one of the best ways to get an overall view of the city before you begin to explore is to go to the corner of **Hradčanské náměstí** (Hradčany Square). From the parapet here you will have a bird's-eye view of the splendid panorama that is Prague, spread out along both sides of the stately River Vltava.

The city is dominated by the cherry-tree covered slopes of

Hradčany hill on which **Pražský hrad** (Prague Castle) rises majestically above the rambling streets of Malá Strana. The Vltava is spanned by several bridges of which the most famous, the 14th-century **Karlův most** (Charles Bridge), leads directly into the heart of Staré Mesto. **Staroměstské náměstí** (Old Town Square) miraculously assimilates a plethora of architectural styles;

the baroque elegance of **Kostel svatého Mikuláše** (St Nicholas's Church) strangely complementing the gaunt angularity of **Marie před Týnem** (Our Lady before Týn), itself partly concealed by the gabled roofs of Gothic and Renaissance houses. The adjoining streets are a living testimony to Prague's rich and glorious past: a maze of half-concealed courtyards and alleyways, of convents and

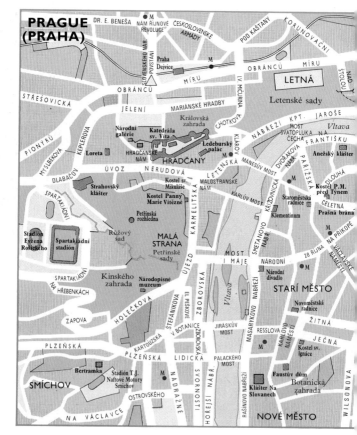

churches, theatres and taverns, shops and houses. A stone's throw away is the former Jewish ghetto of **Josefov**, with its own town hall, synagogues and cemeteries. Prague's most famous street, **Václavské náměstí** (Wenceslas Square) is the focal point of **Nové Město**, actually founded in the Middle Ages. Shops, restaurants and nightclubs predominate here, making it a favourite haunt of locals and visitors alike.

HRADČANY

The city's most important landmarks, **Pražský hrad** (Prague Castle) and **Katedrála svatého Víta** (St Vitus' Cathedral) are situated in Hradčany. The area is especially rich in its architecture and many fine examples can be seen in

St Vitus' Cathedral

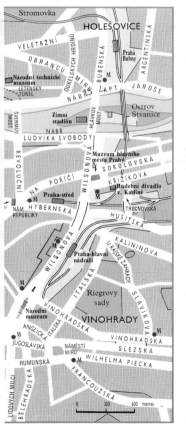

Hradčany Square, a brilliant façade of baroque and classical palaces. Here too is the pilgrimage church of **Loreta** and the picturesque **Nový Svět** (New World) which was formerly the artisan quarter. The stunning interiors of the **Strahovský Klášter** (Strahov Monastery), especially the 18th-century Philosophical Library, home to the **Museum of Czech Literature**, are also a feature of Hradčany.

CENTRAL PRAGUE (PRAHA)

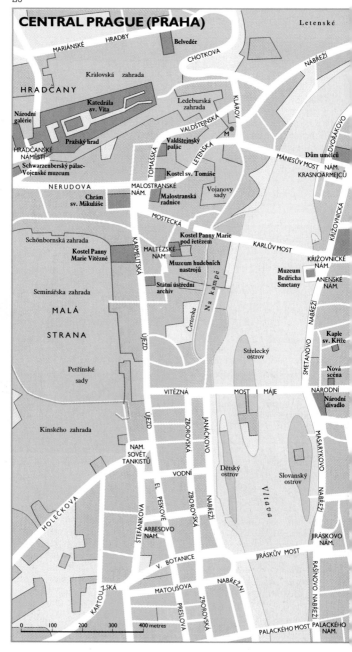

Letenské

MARIÁNSKÉ HRADBY

Belvedér

CHOTKOVA

NÁBŘEŽÍ

Královská zahrada

HRADČANY

Katedrála
sv. Víta

Ledeburská
zahrada

KLÁROV

Národní
galérie

VALDŠTEJNSKÁ

M

DVOŘÁKOVO

Pražský hrad

Valdštejnský
palác

LETENSKÁ

Dům umělců

HRADČANSKÉ
NÁMĚSTÍ

TOMÁŠSKÁ

MÁNESŮV MOST NÁM.
KRASNOARMEJCŮ

Schwarzenberský palác-
Vojenské muzeum

Kostel sv. Tomáše

NERUDOVA

MALOSTRANSKÉ
NÁM.

Vojanovy
sady

Chrám
sv. Mikuláše

Malostranská
radnice

KŘIŽOVNICKÁ

MOSTECKÁ

Schönbornská zahrada

Kostel Panny Marie
pod řetězem

KARLŮV MOST

Kostel Panny
Marie Vítězné

MALTÉZSKÉ
NÁM.

KARMELITSKÁ

Muzeum hudebních
nastrojů

KŘIŽOVNICKÉ
NÁM.

Muzeum
Bedřicha
Smetany

ANENSKÉ
NÁM.

Seminářská zahrada

Státní ústřední
archív

Na kampě

Čertovka

MALÁ

STRANA

NÁBŘEŽÍ

Kaple
sv. Kříže

ÚJEZD

Petřínské
sady

Střelecký
ostrov

SMETANOVO

Nová
scéna

Kinského zahrada

VITĚZNÁ

MOST 1 MÁJE

NÁRODNÍ

Národní
divadlo

ÚJEZD

ZBOROVSKÁ

JANÁČKOVO

NÁM.
SOVĚT.
TANKISTŮ

VODNÍ

Dětský
ostrov

Vltava

Slovanský
ostrov

MASARYKOVO

NÁBŘEŽÍ

EL. PEŠKOVÉ

ZBOROVSKÁ

NÁBŘEŽÍ

HOLEČKOVA

ŠTEFÁNIKOVA

ARBESOVO
NÁM.

JIRÁSKOVO
NÁM.

V. BOTANICE

JIRÁSKŮV MOST

RAŠÍNOVO NÁBŘEŽÍ

KARTOUZSKÁ

MATOUŠOVA

NABŘEŽNÍ

ZBOROVSKÁ

PRESLOVA

0   100   200   300   400 metres

PALACKÉHO MOST PALACKÉHO
NÁM.

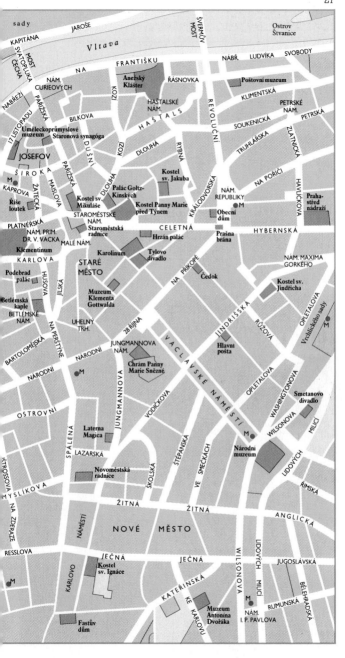

◆◆
ČERNÍN PALACE
Loretánské náměstí,
Stretching the entire length of
Loretánské náměstí (Loretánska
Square), a distance of 160 yards
(154 m), is the uniform grey
Černín Palace. This imposing
edifice, formerly the residence
of the Imperial ambassador to
Venice, now houses the Czech
Ministry of Foreign Affairs. In
March 1948 the sole surviving
non-Communist member of the
government, Jan Masaryk, son of
the founder of modern
Czechoslovakia, was found dead

Loretánské náměstí

in the palace courtyard. The
official verdict was suicide;
however, it is widely believed
that Masaryk was murdered on
the orders of Stalin.

◆◆◆
HRADČANSKÉ NÁMĚSTI (HRADČANY SQUARE)
Tram: nos 22, 23
Metro: Hradčanská
Hradčany Square stands at the
approach to Prague Castle and
formed part of the processional
route at the coronations of the
kings of Bohemia. At the centre
of the original town of Hradčany,
this square underwent massive
reconstruction after the fire of

Rococo façade, Archbishop's Palace

1541. Originally it was lined with burghers' houses but after the fire it became the site of palaces for the nobility and church dignitaries. In the centre stands a baroque Plague column with a statue of the Virgin Mary with the eight Patron saints of the land and, nearby, a decorative cast-iron candelabrum from the 19th century – a relic of the days of gas lighting. It was here too that, in August 1547, the leaders of the anti-Habsburg rebellion were executed.

The recently restored **Archbishop's Palace** (no 16) was originally a Renaissance palace built for Florián Gryspek of Gryspach before 1538. Later Ferdinand I bought it and presented it to the first post-Hussite Catholic Archbishop of Prague, Antonin Brus of Mohelnice. The palace was rebuilt between 1562–4. Over a century later, between 1675 and 1688, it was remodelled in baroque style by the French architect Jean-Baptiste Mathey.

Mathey's magnificent marble doorway is virtually all that remains, as in 1764 work began on construction of the present stunning, rococo façade. Johann Joseph Wirch was the architect of this final reconstruction and was also responsible for much of the lavish interior decoration. The façade itself is richly decorated with stucco works and adorned with the magnificent and sizeable family crest of Archbishop Anton Peter Graf, Prince of Prichowitz. Below this are sculptures by I F Platzer and the later works of T Seidan can be seen.

Inside are further fine stucco decorations, wood carvings and a collection of glass and porcelain although the public are only admitted once a year on Maundy Thursday.

Next to the Archbishop's Palace at no 15 is the **Sternberg Palace**, now part of the **National Gallery** (see **Národní Galérie**, page 34) which houses the main collection of European Art, and is also the venue of occasional temporary exhibitions. This 18th-century palace was designed by Alliprandi, who based his designs on works by the Viennese architect Martinelli. It has fine ceiling paintings and frescos.

On the south side of the square at no 2 and opposite the Sternberg Palace is the **Schwarzenberg Palace and Museum of Military History**; it ranks with the castle and the Archbishop's Palace as one of the finest buildings in the area. The site was acquired by Jan of Lobkowicz after the fire in 1541, and soon after, he

Ceiling, Schwarzenberg Palace

commissioned a large palace to be built on the area. Mainly remarkable for its distinctive, but much restored, sgraffito decoration and projecting cornices in the style of North Italian models, it is a good example of Renaissance palace architecture in Prague. Late 16th-century frescos adorn the ceiling in the main hall on the second floor and in some other rooms. These include illustrations of allegorical figures and scenes from Homer's poems: 'The Trial of Paris'; 'The Abduction of Helen'; 'The Conquering of Troy' and the 'Flight of Aeneas from burning Troy'. It wasn't until 1719, after the palace had changed ownership three more times that it was acquired by the Schwarzenberg family. The neighbouring Empire-style **Salm Palace** was bought by Joseph Schwarzenberg in 1811, who then connected it with the main Schwarzenberg Palace. A large letter 'S' adorned with a crown is found on the grille of the gate to the former Salm Palace, after Archbishop Vilém Florentin of Salm, who built the palace in the early 19th century. These days this part of the building is the home of the Swiss Embassy.
At the top of the square, on the corner of Loretánská, is the yellow fronted **Tuscany Palace**, so called because in the early 18th century it belonged to the Duke of Tuscany. His sculptured coat of arms can be seen above the two columned portals. This two-storey edifice was probably built by the French architect Jean Mathey between 1689 and 1691 for Michel Osvald Thun-

Tuscany Palace's Italianate façade

Hohenstein. It was not until 1718 that the palace was acquired by the dukes of Tuscany. Today it is the property of the Czech Foreign Minister. The harmonious proportions of its early baroque façade (restored after 1945), decorated with statuary and stucco work, are very attractive.
Standing at the north-west corner of the square is the handsome Renaissance **Martinic Palace**. It was originally designed at the end of the 16th century and in 1624 Jaroslav Bořita von Martinice acquired the palace. (He was one of the two Imperial councillors who suffered defenestration in 1618.) Martinice commissioned an extra storey to be added together with the Renaissance

gables and the coat of arms set above the main entrance. In 1971, during restoration work, a band of fine 16th- and early 17th-century sgraffito decoration was newly uncovered on the façade which faces the square. It depicts Biblical scenes including Joseph's Flight from Putiphar. On the façade facing the inner courtyards there are scenes from the life of Samson and of Hercules. The interior of the palace offers a chance to see an exceptionally complicated coffered ceiling (in the main hall) and copper beam ceilings with vegetable and figural motifs. Today this palace is the headquarters and residence of the capital's Chief Architect and it is also the venue for exhibitions, concerts and literary recitals.

No 10 Hradčany Square was the home of Peter Parler, the famous builder who was responsible for St Vitus's Cathedral. In the early 18th century the house was connected with its neighbour, **No 9**, by a richly decorated baroque façade.

There are several canonical houses in the square which can be identified by the coat of arms of the St Vitus Chapter: a gold band in a black field. At **No 3** is the **Monastery of the Barnabites**. An early baroque edifice built on the site of the original presbytery of the Church of St Benedictine, it was given to the Barnabite Order in 1626. In 1784 the monastery was abolished but soon after awarded to the Mendicant Carmelites. In 1958 the building was converted into a hotel for guests of the state.

The Church of St Benedict, the parish church of the medieval town of Hradčany, was originally Gothic. Rebuilt in the late 15th century and again after 1541, the present baroque building was constructed in the 17th century and modified in the early 18th century. The furnishings inside also date from the 18th century.

◆◆◆
LORETA (LORETO SHRINE)
Loretánské náměstí
Trams: 22, 23

The cream-coloured building with the green spire opposite the Černín Palace is the Loreto Shrine, a religious foundation dating back to the time of the Counter-Reformation. According to a 13th-century legend the Holy Family's Home in Nazareth (Casa Santa) was transported to Loreto in Italy to protect it against non-believers. The cult which then grew up around the legend spread to the Eastern European countries in the mid-15th century and some fifty Loreto shrines were built in Bohemia, a propaganda exercise to influence the Czechs.

The architectural and spiritual centre of this place of pilgrimage is the **Loretánská Kaple** (Loreto Chapel). Commissioned by Countess Benigna Kateřina of Lobkowicz it was built between 1626 and 1631 by the Italian architect Giovanni Orsi. The legend of the shrine is depicted on its east wall, while elsewhere there are sculpture and stucco reliefs to illustrate the Lives of Mary and Old Testament Prophets. Originally the building was painted on the outside; it wasn't until 1664 that the stucco

Loretánská Kaple, Prague's Loreto

and sculptural reliefs were added by Italian artists.

Inside the Prague Loreto building there are several bricks and beams said to have come from the Italian Loreto. Whether or not this is true the baroque interior of the **Casa Santa** is sumptuous and features pictures from the *Life of the Virgin Mary* by František Kunz, a silver altar and a fine carved *Madonna*. This is framed by some magnificent silver decoration attributed to the Prague goldsmith Markus Hrbek.

The Casa Santa stands behind an 18th-century façade and within the confines of a two-storeyed cloister. It is flanked by two fountains, one depicting *Mary's Ascension into Heaven* and the other the *Resurrection of Our Lord*. Originally both were the work of Brüderle dating from 1739 and 1740, but the first is now a copy.

The façade, designed by Christoph and Kilian Deintzenhofer (father and son), was built between 1720 and 1722. Strangely, its bell tower dates from the late 17th century and contains a carillon of 27 bells cast in Amsterdam for a wealthy merchant. Their total weight is approximately 3,380 lbs (1,540 kg) and each hour a Marian song rings out, although other tunes can be played on the bells by means of an electronic keyboard in the steeple.

The **Cloisters** which date from a little later than the shrine itself were originally built with only one storey; the second was added in about 1740. On the first floor there are mid-18th-century frescos by F Scheffler depicting themes from the Marian Litany. Each of the seven chapels which border the cloisters feature fine paintings and adornments.

On the east side is the **Church of the Nativity of Our Lord**, begun in 1717 and completed in 1735. A delicate painting of 'Christ in the Temple' by V Reiner decorates the sacristy ceiling but the High Altar and the altarpiece by J Heintsch of the birth of Christ dominates the interior. J Schöpf, the principal of the Prague Guild of Artists, painted the frescos ('Adoration of the Shepherds' and 'Adoration of the Three Magi' in 1742.

On the upper floor in the western part of the cloister is the **Treasury**, which was restored in 1984. Apart from the vestments and other liturgical items the display exhibits some fabulous monstrances dating from the 16th to the 18th centuries. The Pearl Monstrance is decorated with a ruby, pearls and 266 diamonds; the Ring Monstrance is adorned with 492 diamonds, 186 rubies, a sapphire, pearls, emeralds, amethysts and garnets but the most breathtaking of all is the famous Diamond Monstrance. Made in Vienna in 1699, it glitters with no less than 6,200 diamonds.

Open: Tuesday to Sunday 09.00 to 12.00 hrs and 13.00 to 17.00 hrs.
Closed: Monday.

◆◆◆
NARODNÍ GALÉRIE, ŠTERNBERSKY PALÁC (NATIONAL GALLERY, STERNBERG PALACE)

Hradčanské náměstí 15
Most of the major Western European schools are represented in this impressive collection which is housed on the first and second floors of a 17th-century baroque palace, tucked away behind the Archbishop's Palace in Hradčany Square. The first floor concentrates on Italian Renaissance painting of the 14th and 15th centuries and includes works by Andrea Della Robbia, Sebastiano del Piombo and Piero della Francesca. The Dutch and Flemish schools of the 15th and 16th centuries are represented by the likes of Geertgen tot Sint Jans and the Brueghels, father and son. The second floor embraces European painting of the 14th to 18th centuries, with artists like Dürer, Tintoretto, Veronese, Rubens and Rembrandt.

A separate exhibition across the courtyard focuses on 19th- and 20th-century French painting. As well as works by the major Impressionists – Monet, Renoir, Cézanne, Gauguin and van Gogh – there are some outstanding modern paintings by Matisse, Chagall, Braque and Picasso.

Open: Tuesday to Sunday 10.00 to 18.00 hrs.
Closed: Monday.

NATIONAL MUSEUM OF CZECH LITERATURE (see STRAHOVSKÝ KLÁŠTER)

◆◆
NOVÝ SVĚT (NEW WORLD)

Just beyond the Loreto Shrine is one of the prettiest little corners of old Prague, Nový svět. This quarter of Hradčany was originally built in the 16th century on a track which led from Prague to Střešovice. The great astronomer Johannes Kepler stayed at the house U zlatého noha (At the Golden Fairy Bird), no. 1 in 1600. Also look out for U Zlaté hrušky (At the Golden Pear) at no. 3, which is now a wine bar.

Ceremonial courtyard, Pražský hrad

◆◆◆
PRAŽSKÝ HRAD
(PRAGUE CASTLE)

Tram: no. 22 from the National Theatre to U Praného mostů
Metro: Malostranská

On foot, take the flight of steps called Zámecké schody, a steep climb, but well worth it for the views across Prague and because it leads directly into Hradčanské náměstí. Another, more picturesque flight of steps Staré zámecké schody, approaches the eastern end of the castle complex from the vicinity of the metro station. There have been several castles on this site. Prince Bořivoj, the first documented ruler of the Přemyslid dynasty, built a wooden fortress here in the 9th century. After its destruction in 1041, the castle was rebuilt and enlarged. This Romanesque structure comprised massive stone fortifications, palaces for the king and bishop, two monasteries and several churches including the **Bazilika svatého Jiří** (St George's Basilica) which still survives.

The subsequent history is a colourful tale of sieges, burnings, floods and other disasters, until the Gothic castle was completed in about 1420. Its centrepiece was the **Katedrála svatého Víta** (Cathedral of St Vitus). The administrative importance of the castle declined as Bohemia gradually succumbed to Austrian influence in the course of the 17th century. In 1753, the Empress Maria Theresa ordered a reconstruction on neoclassical lines, a transformation which gives the castle its present, chateau-like appearance. It was completed in 1775.

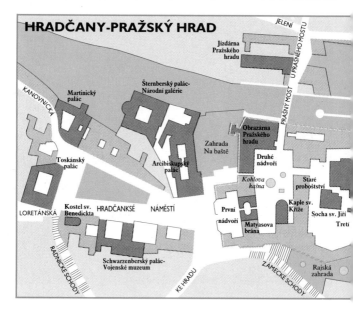

HRADČANY-PRAŽSKÝ HRAD

Standing to attention outside the main entrance are two members of the Hradní stráž (Castle Guard). Their blue uniforms are a recent innovation, replacing the khaki of the former Communist regime. Guarding the guardians on either side of a delicate wrought-iron gateway are two massive stone titans, giving short shrift to their enemies.

The **První nádvoří** (First or Ceremonial Courtyard) was built over the original castle moat. It was built between 1756 and 1774 during the reign of Empress Maria Theresa. Straight ahead is the **Matyasova brána** (Matthias Gate) originally separate, but now integrated into the palace façade. It dates from 1614. The oversized flags on either side proclaim that inside are the

Arms and the man – a castle guard

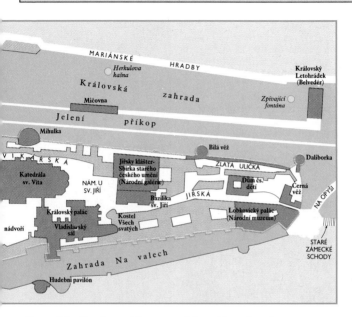

offices of the Czech president.
Encased in a Renaissance grille
in the centre of the **Druhé
nádvoří** (Second Courtyard) is a
well dating from the 17th
century. Off to the right is the
rounded apse of the former
Kaple svatého Kříže (Holy Cross
Chapel) now the cathedral
Treasury. Open to the public, it
contains various reliquaries and
other sacred objects including
crucifixes and jewelled cups.
The courtyard itself originated in
the latter half of the 16th century
but its present appearance dates
from the reign of Maria Theresa.
Hradní Galérie (Castle Gallery)
on the left, houses paintings from
the collection of the Emperor
Rudolph II and others. Works by
Titian, Tintoretto, Veronese and
Rubens as well as the Bohemian
baroque artists Jan Kupecký and

Johann Peter Brand.
Open: Tuesday to Sunday 10.00
to 18.00 hrs.
Closed: Monday.
An unobtrusive passageway
leads into the **Tretí nádvoří**
(Third Courtyard). The pink-
fronted building with the granite
base and steps is the **Staré
proboštsví** (Old Provost's
Residence) which contains the
ruins of the Romanesque
Bishop's Palace.
Directly ahead through the
passageway is the richly
embroidered façade of **St Vitus
Cathedral**. The Cathedral is
probably the finest building in
the Hradčany and is also
Prague's largest church. It is
over 407 feet (124 metres long)
and rises to 108 feet (33 metres)
above the nave, the roof is
supported by 28 piers and there

are 21 chapels.

There have been three churches on this site: the first, no more than a chapel, was founded by Prince Wenceslas in 925; the second, a substantial Romanesque basilica with double choir was completed in the following century; the present Gothic structure was begun by Charles IV in 1344. The distinguished German architect Peter Parler and his two sons were responsible for the lofty choir and the surrounding chapels, which were completed early in the 15th

Above: commanding the river Vltava, Pražský hrad dominates the night. Left: gate, Katedrála svatého Víta

century. Between 1560 and 1562 the tower was capped with a Renaissance steeple, to which baroque embellishments were later added. The western end of the cathedral (the work of J Mocker and K Hilbert) is of much more recent origin and was not completed until 1929. Enter the Cathedral by the south porch at the side of the building. Known as the Golden Portal, it is

the work of Peter Parler and dates from 1347. The intricate mosaic depicting the Last Judgement is by 14th-century Italian artists and features Charles IV and his wife Eliška. It is currently being restored. (Note also the gilded Renaissance window on the tower.)

Immediately to the right of the doorway is the exquisite Chapel of St Wenceslas. Conceived by Peter Parler, 1358 to 1367, the lower walls are encrusted with semi-precious stones and decorated with a Passion Cycle by Master Oswald of Prague.

The Renaissance paintings on the upper walls are by an unknown Master and depict the life of St Wenceslas, whose tomb lies beneath the altar. Also noteworthy are the 14th-century statue of the saint under the east window and the wooden doorway, decorated with a 13th-century lion's head.

The Chapel of the Holy Rood, or Cross, leads directly into the Crypt. Supports and capitals of the earlier Romanesque church are displayed here, alongside the sarcophagi of the rulers of the Přemyslid dynasty. Explore the remainder of the Cathedral at your leisure. You will find everything from delicate Gothic stonework (see especially the Vladislav Oratory) to finely detailed baroque woodcarving in the choir. Modern artists are also well represented, particularly in the stained glass windows of the nave. Of particular note is the traceried window by Max Svabinský erected in 1934 to depict the Last Judgement. It contains 40,000 pieces of glass.

In the centre of the Third Courtyard is a statue of St George. The original was cast in 1373 by Jiří and Martin of Cluj and can now be found in the Monastery of St George. Before joining the queue for the Royal Palace (see below) have a look at the excavated remains of the medieval fortifications and earthworks, discovered in 1920 and preserved beneath a green-roofed shelter adjoining the old Bishop's Palace.

The 18th-century façade of the **Královský palác** (Royal Palace) is deceptive, for it conceals a multi-levelled network of halls and chambers belonging to earlier palaces, which provide a fascinating insight into life at the Bohemian court. To the left of the entrance is the Green Chamber, an audience hall from the time of Charles IV. A flight of steps lead to Vadislav's Bedchamber. Vadislav is Vadislav Jagiello, who united Bohemia with the kingdoms of Poland and Hungary at the end of the 15th century. His monogram (the letter W) can be seen above the window, opposite the Polish emblem of the eagle and crown. Note the fine Gothic vault. Return to the entrance and directly in front of you is the imposing Vadislav Hall, built by Benedikt Rieth between 1493 and 1502. This was the throne room where, traditionally, the kings of Bohemia received the oath of allegiance from their princely subjects. It was also a suitably splendid setting for coronation feasts, assemblies, even tournaments. Through the doorway to the right are the rooms of the Bohemian Chancellery. The first room contains a model of the castle as it was in the 18th century. Passing through a Renaissance portal into the second room, you will note Czech visitors gathering around a window overlooking the gardens. It was from here, in May 1618, that two hated Catholic ministers and a clerk were hurled into the moat below. They survived but the incident, known as the 'Second Defenestration of Prague', sparked off a rising against the Habsburgs which led to the Thirty Years War. Above this room is the Hall of the Imperial Court Council containing portraits of the Habsburg rulers from the 16th to the 18th centuries. Access is via a spiral staircase. The steps at the far end of the Vladislav Hall lead to a gallery overlooking All Saints Chapel. Unfortunately, few traces of its 14th-century origins remain. A narrow passageway to the side of the chapel affords access to an observation terrace, from where there is a fine view of Prague. The doorway opposite leads to the Diet Hall, originally part of Charles IV's palace. Its present Renaissance appearance dates from 1559–63. More portraits of the Habsburgs adorn the walls. The Royal Throne is 19th century. Next to the Diet, the Riders' Staircase, so called because it was designed especially to be used by knights on horseback entering the hall for tournaments, leads to the remains of the Gothic Palace (not always accessible). The main points of interest here are The Charles Hall, with its fine medieval vaulting and the Romanesque Princes Palace. The church with the orange baroque façade, overlooking Jiřské náměstí (St George's Square) is the **Bazilika svatého Jiří** (Basilica of St George). The surprise here is the wonderfully preserved Romanesque interior, restored during renovation work between 1897 and 1907 and again 1959–62. It is the oldest church in the castle and the 12th-

century Basilica and the convent which adjoins it – actually the first in Bohemia – formed part of the original Hradčany. The perfect symmetry of the architecture is matched by the breathtaking ceiling paintings from the 13th century which adorn the apse. The Ludmilla Chapel is decorated with the work of Renaissance artists – also of very high quality. The chapel contains the tomb of St Ludmilla, one of Czechoslovakia's patron saints. There is no direct access but you can see into the chapel through a grille. Below the main altar is the crypt, not always open to visitors.

The Basilica of St George

The Convent of St George, with its outstanding Romanesque tower contains a fascinating exhibition of the National Gallery's Bohemian art collection (see page 34).

Children will love the colourful little cottages and cobblestones of **Zlatá Ulička** (Golden Lane) which back onto the Castle walls. The houses originally belonged to archers and goldsmiths serving the court in the second half of the 16th century. Franz Kafka, Czechoslovakia's most famous prose writer, once lived at no. 22.

There are souvenir shops galore and, at the end of the street, a charming café called Vl. Zlaté Ulička (not too restful however; the whole area gets rather crowded).

Before leaving the Castle complex via Vikářská (on the north side of St Vitus Cathedral), take a look at the Powder Tower. Cannon were once stored here and the place later served as a laboratory, housing the equipment for the Imperial alchemists.

Hradčány's own antidote to splendour

SBÍRKA STARÉHO ČESKÉHO UMENÍ (COLLECTION OF OLD BOHEMIAN ART)
Jiřsky klástěr
Religious treasures from Bohemia's Medieval past – mainly panel paintings and altarpieces – are on show in the former Convent of St George, Prague Castle. They include the

14th-century cycle painted by Master Theodoric for the Holy Cross Chapel in Karlštejn Castle. The first floor is devoted to the work of baroque artists ranging from Mannerism through to the end of the 18th century and includes examples by Karel Škréta and Johannes Kupetzky. *Open:* April to November Tuesday to Sunday 10.00 to 18.00 hrs. *Closed:* Monday.

◆◆◆
STRAHOVSKÝ KLÁŠTER (THE STRAHOV MONASTERY)
Strahovské nadvorí 132
Trams: 22, 23
The Strahov Monastery was founded in 1140 by Prince Vladislav II. This Premonstratensian monastery, Prague's second oldest religious house, stands on Petřín Hill overlooking the Malá Strana valley and in 1360, when the Hunger Wall was built around Hradčany, it was incorporated into the boundaries of the town. Few traces of its early history remain for the visitor to see today (there are three preserved Romanesque rooms in the western part of the convent); the building has undergone a good deal of building, restyling and reconstruction down through the centuries. During the battles between the French and Austrian armies in 1741 it suffered severe damage. Much of its present appearance is the result of the reconstruction that consequently took place. What draws most visitors to this place are the magnificent libraries which form part of

the **Pamatnik Narodního Písemnictví** (Museum of Czech Literature). The two library halls, the Theological Hall and the Philosophical Hall, were built nearly a century apart; the Theological Hall in 1671 by Giovanni Orsi and the Philosophical Hall in 1783 by the architect I Palliardi. Both house parts of the huge collection that represents literary development from as early as the 9th century until the 18th century. Over 130,000 volumes, 2,500 early printed books (incunabula) and 5,000 manuscripts are kept here; included among the numerous literary curiosities are books prohibited over the centuries by the Catholic Church. Don't expect to see too many lurid covers however! One of the most valuable manuscripts is the 9th/10th-century Strahov Gospel Book, still one of the oldest in existence in Central Europe. The Strahov Herbarium, a Latin dictionary and medical books date back to the 15th century and large stocks of books from many Bohemian religious houses dissolved after the World War II have also found their way into the Strahov Library.
Visitors to the museum can also see a reconstructed 17th-century printing press. It was during the librarianship of J B Dlabač (1758–1820) that the monastery gained its reputation as a centre of Czech education and culture. Quite apart from the astounding literary collection, both library halls are architectural masterpieces. The walls of the vast 46 foot (14m)-high Philosophical Hall, the most famous of Prague's neoclassical

monuments, are lined with finely carved bookcases by J Lachovfer, brought here from the abolished Premonstratensian monastery Bruch Abbey in Southern Moravia. Its ceiling is decorated with a stunning rococo fresco by A Maulpertsch (1794). S Nosecký, a Strahov monk, painted the ceiling frescos in the earlier Theological Hall between 1723 and 1727; a series of 17th-century geographical and astral globes are displayed in this room.

Before it was abolished in 1784, the parish church of Strahov was the Church of St Roch which stands in the forecourt of the monastery complex. Mozart played the organ here.

Poetry readings, concerts and temporary exhibitions are now regular features of the museum.
Open: Tuesday to Sunday 09.00 to 17.00 hrs.
Closed: Monday.

Painted vault of the Theological Hall, Strahovský klášter

VOJENSKÉ MUZEUM (MILITARY HISTORY MUSEUM)
Schwarzenbersky palác, Hradčanské náměstí
An opportunity to see the interior of this fine Renaissance palace. The military history of Czechoslovakia from the year dot to the end of the World War I is covered in this vast exhibition of weapons, uniforms and all things martial.
Open: May to October, Tuesday to Friday 09.00–15.30 hrs; Saturday and Sunday 09.00–17.00 hrs.
Closed: Monday.
A separate exhibition in the annex at U Památniku 2, Praha 3 covers the history of the Czech armies of World Wars I and II.
Open: Tuesday to Sunday 09.30 to 16.30 hrs.
Closed: Monday.

MALÁ STRANA

Below the castle area is Malá
Strana (Lesser Town), which
developed as a suburb for the
aristocracy; hence the grand
17th- and 18th-century palaces
and gardens, churches and
monasteries. There are also
smaller but no less attractive
houses built by burghers and
artisans. The **Malostranské
náměstí** (Lesser Town Square)
was the centre of life in this area
as early as the 10th century.
Today it is lined with palaces
and grand houses and at its
centre, **Chrám svatého Mikuláše**
(St Nicholas's Church),
considered to be one of the
finest baroque structures north of
the Alps and the epitome of
Bohemian baroque. From here
the Mostecká leads you to the
14th-century **Karlův most**
(Charles Bridge) another of
Prague's major sights. Until 1841
it was the only bridge in Prague
to cross the Vltava.
Look out also for the **British
Embassy** in Thunovská. This
magnificent baroque palace was
built in 1716–27 on the site of an
earlier building belonging to the
Archbishop of Salzburg. Mozart
and his wife stayed here on their
first visit to Prague in January
1787. The distinctive turreted
gateway, decorated with the
royal insignia of the lion and
unicorn, was added in 1850.
The first sessions of the
Czechoslovak National
Assembly, after the declaration
of independence in November
1918, were held in the Diet
building in **Sněmovní** (no. 4).
Neighbouring **Tomášská**, with
baroque and classical façades,

is a delight to stroll in. The
Valdštejnská hospoda, one of
Prague's most fashionable
restaurants, is at the corner of
Valdštejnský náměstí.

Baroque poses, Karlův most

◆◆◆
KARLŮV MOST (CHARLES
BRIDGE)
*Metro: Staromestská,
Malostranská*
Trams: 12, 17, 18, 22
For more than a thousand years,
a bridge has spanned the River
Vltava on or about this point.
When the first stone crossing,
known as the Judith Bridge, was
swept away by flood water in the
manner of its wooden
predecessor, King Charles IV
decided that enough was

Malá Strana gate from Karlův most

enough. In 1357, he commissioned Peter Parler, architect of St Vitus Cathedral, to build the massive Gothic structure which still stands today. It was completed early in the 15th century, in the reign of Wenceslas IV. The flamboyant sculptures which decorate the parapets and give the bridge its characteristic appearance are a baroque afterthought. This cannot be said of the formidable Staré Město Bridge Tower, which dates from 1391. The three figures carved in stone above the archway represent St Vitus, flanked by the two great monarchs of the 14th century, Charles IV and Wenceslas IV. Throughout the Middle Ages, the bridge buzzed with business and commercial traffic. Justice was administered here: convicted felons were lowered from the piers in wicker baskets, before embarking on a watery sentence. Tournaments were held, and processions passed by en route to the Castle. The view from the bridge – of the Vltava and its shady banks, of the rooftops and spires of the Malá Strana, and of the majestic slopes of Castle Hill, crowned by the cathedral, will compel you to linger. Take a closer look at the sculptures too. The first to appear was the bronze crucifix, third in line on the right hand side. Cast in 1629, it was erected in 1657. The inscription on the tablet is in Hebrew and was paid for by a wealthy Jewish citizen accused of blasphemy. The majority of the statues are 18th century, though not all are original. The bronze image of St John of Nepomuk, erected in 1683, shows him carrying a crucifix, his head ringed by a starry halo. His right to a place can scarcely be disputed, for in 1393 he was bound in chains and hurled from this very spot – dire punishment for siding with his archbishop against the king. At the far end of the bridge is the Malá Strana gateway. The smaller of the two fortified towers was originally part of the 12th-century Judith Bridge – its present appearance is the result of a Renaissance facelift. The higher tower was build in 1464 and replaced an earlier Romanesque bastion. Immediately in front of the gateway is the former customs house, a reminder of the days when the Malá Strana was a separate town. Straight ahead is **Mostecká**, now a busy shopping street. The large yellow building at no. 3, with the peacock sign outside, is the Saxon House, so called because it was presented by Charles IV to Rudolph, Duke of Saxony in the 14th century. Opposite, at no. 4, is the House at Saviour's, really two baroque houses joined together. Above one of the first floor windows is an 18th-century relief of a bear.

◆
KARMELITSKÁ ULICE (CARMELITE STREET)
Trams: 12, 22
The building with the distinctive octagonal dome is the former **Klášter svatého Maří Magdalény** (Convent of St Mary Magdalene) (currently undergoing restoration). Hopefully more of the original Gothic church, demolished in 1420, will be uncovered. The present baroque structure dates from 1656–77. Both convent and church were secularised towards the end of the 18th century; the convent functioning for a while as a post office and then as a police barracks. It now houses the **Czechoslovak Historical Archive**.
The undistinguished and rather gloomy **Kostel Panny Marie Vítězné** (Church of Our Lady of Victories) is famous only for its statue of the Holy Infant of Prague. The beautifully robed wax figure was brought here from Spain in the middle of the 16th century. The church was originally a Lutheran foundation, but was handed over to the Carmelite Order in 1624.

◆◆◆
MALOSTRANSKÉ NÁMĚSTÍ (LESSER TOWN SQUARE)

Metro: Malostranká
Trams: 12, 22

Actually two squares, separated by the domed **Chrám svatého Mikuláše** (church of St Nicholas) which presides over the entire district. This monument to the high baroque style was built over the foundations of an earlier Gothic church, dating from 1283. In 1625 it was presented by Ferdinand II to the Jesuits, who commissioned the present building from Christoph Dientzenhofer. He built the towering nave and side chapels but the dome and choir are the work of his son, Kilian. The church was finally completed in 1756.

Some of the ceiling frescos are on a gargantuan scale – J L Kracker's painting in the nave, covering an area of more than 1,794 square yards (1,500 sq m), is reckoned to be one of the largest in Europe. *Open:* daily, November to February 09.00 to 16.00 hrs; March and April 09.00 to 17.00 hrs; May to September 09.00 to 18.00 hrs; October 10.00 to 17.00 hrs.

The barrack-like building adjoining the church is the former **Jesuit College** (note their

The nave, Chrám svatého Mikuláše

The church's baroque exterior

IHS motto over the door).
On the east side of the lower square (no. 21) is the small, but stately **Malostranská radnice** (Lesser Town Hall). This handsome building from the late Renaissance was the focal point of the municipality until 1784, when the Malá Strana merged with Prague proper. Advertising banners draped across the arcade now spoil the harmonious symmetry of the whole. Two houses combine to form the baroque house **At the Flavins** (no. 22). Its distinguishing feature is a prettily painted fresco depicting the Annunciation of Our Lady. The building is named after the original owner, Vít Flavin, a Czech humanist of the Renaissance. Next door is the **Kaiserstein Palace**, which dates from 1700. The statues above the attic represent the four seasons. The present palace was formerly two buildings and these were

mentioned as early as the 15th century. Their Gothic cellars have been preserved. From 1907 the palace was owned by Ema Destinnová (1878–1930) the famous soprano and partner of Enrico Caruso. There is a bust of her on the façade.

The spire of **Kostel svatého Tomáše** (St Thomas's Church) rises above the rooftops on this side of the square and provides an interesting architectural contrast. The entrance is in Letenská. Of medieval origins, the present building, with its severe baroque façade, is the work of Kilian Dietzenhofer, who also designed the dome of St Nicholas (see above). Peter Paul Rubens was commissioned to produce the paintings of St Augustine (the church was an Augustinian monastery) and St Thomas, but the versions you see in the nave today are copies – the originals are in the National Gallery (see page 34). Also dedicated to the memory of St Thomas is the fine old restaurant, **U svatého Tomáše** (entrance in Letenská 12).

The cream and grey building opposite the entrance to St Nicholas's Church, in what is known as the upper part of Lesser Town Square, is the **Lichtenstein Palace**. It skillfully integrates five merchants' houses which were bought up by Jan of Lobkowicz in 1591. Thirty years later, the palace passed into the hands of Karel of Lichtenstein. The neoclassical façade is late 18th century. In the centre of the square is a Plague Column, erected in 1715 to commemorate the ending of an epidemic.

MALTÉZSKÉ NÁMĚSTÍ (MALTESE SQUARE)

The square can best be approached from Lázeňská (starting from Mostecká, the first street on the left). The building at the far end (no. 4) is the **Convent of the Order of Maltese Knights**, now the Czechoslovak Academy of Sciences. (Note the Maltese Cross on the main door and under the roof.) The house at no. 6 was once a hotel. Peter the Great stayed here on one occasion as did the French poet René Chateaubriand. To the left of the entrance next door is a plaque commemorating the fact that Beethoven lived here in 1796.

The **Kostel Panny Marie pod řetězem** (Church of Our Lady Below the Chain) was once part of the monastery complex of the Maltese Knights. The foundation dates from 1169 and traces of the original Romanesque buildings can still be seen in the courtyard, behind the two Early Gothic towers (1389). The church was reconstructed in the 17th century and the artwork of the interior dates mainly from this period. Next door is the **Museum of Musical Instruments** (see below).

Maltese Square runs off to the right. On the corner at no. 11 is the house **At the Painters**. Renaissance in spirit (it was built in 1531) it is now one of the most sought-after restaurants in Prague, u Malířů. Of the many outstanding buildings in the square, the **Palais Turba** (no. 6, with the brilliant white and pink façade) is possibly the finest. Constructed in rococo style in

1767, it is now the Japanese Embassy. Also look out for the **Nostitz Palace** (no. 1). This huge baroque edifice was designed in the years 1658–60 for the Nostitz family. Some of the external details are rococo additions. The palace is now the premises of the Dutch Embassy.

MUZEUM HUDEBNÍCH NÁSTROJU (MUSEUM OF MUSICAL INSTRUMENTS)
Lázeňská 2

Situated in the heart of Malá Strana, the museum boasts an outstanding collection of old keyboard instruments: handsomely crafted clavichords, harpsichords and early pianofortes dating from the 18th and 19th centuries. (Incidentally, Beethoven stayed at no. 11 Lázeňská while on a visit to Prague in 1796.)
Open: (summer only) Tuesday to Sunday 10.00 to 16.00 hrs.
Closed: Monday.

NA KAMPĚ

Leading away to the east of Maltese Square, at the end of Velkopřevor náměstí, is the islet known as Na Kampě. Separated from the Malá Strana proper by the Čertovka or Devil's Stream, it is a secluded world of its own, with stately period houses, waterways, parks and gardens. From the late 16th century Na Kampě became known for its pottery markets. Ceramics from the Beroun region and the Vltava valley were sold here. This tradition is still continued by the shops selling Czech ceramics here.

Off the beaten track, Na Kampě

◆◆
NERUDOVA
Tram: 12, 20, 22
Winding its way up to the Castle from the Malostranské náměstí Nerudova is a quiet neighbourhood of shops, houses and restaurants, all very attractive. Look out particularly for the house signs: the Cat (no. 2), now a beer bar, the Red Eagle (no. 6), the Three Fiddles (no. 12), currently a wine bar, the Golden Cup (no. 16), the Devil wine bar, and St John of Nepomuk (no. 18). No. 20 is the **Thun-Hohenstein Palace**, now the Italian Embassy. Like many of the buildings in this street, it dates originally from the 16th century. If you have worked up a thirst, the beer bar Bonaparta is at no. 29 or, if you prefer something non-alcoholic, there is an expresso bar next door. Nerudova continues as Úvoz. This was once a suburb outside the fortified walls of the castle. The houses here are a treat,

especially At the Three Magi (no. 2), referred to as far back as the 14th century, and At the Three Small Axes (no. 6). The climb up the hill is well worth the effort, as the view from the top is magnificent, taking in the Strahov Monastery (see page 43), the gardens of the Malá Strana and the less aesthetically pleasing Petřín Tower modelled on the Eiffel Tower and erected for the Prague Industrial Exhibition of 1891. Tram no. 22 will take you back into town.

◆◆
VALDŠTEJNSKÝ PALÁC (WALLENSTEIN PALACE AND GARDENS)
Valdštejnské náměstí
Metro: Malostranská,
Trams: 12, 22
The sedate baroque residence at the corner of the square originally belonged to Albrecht of Wallenstein (1583–1634), one

Zahrada Valdstejnského Palác

of the greatest generals of the
Thirty Years War. A
swashbuckling figure with a
thirst for wealth and personal
aggrandisement, he successfully
campaigned against the
Protestant armies of Denmark,
Saxony and Sweden before
finally succumbing to the blow of
an assassin's axe – dire
punishment for intriguing against
his Habsburg master, the
Emperor Ferdinand II. More
than two dozen houses were
demolished to make way for the
palace, which was erected by a
team of Italian architects in the
years 1624–30. The buildings
remained in the hands of the
Wallenstein family until the end
of World War II, when it was
acquired by the state. It is not
generally open to the public.
Zahrada Valdstejnského Palác
(the Gardens), on the other hand,

are accessible (through an
entrance in Letenská) and some
would say these are the palace's
most attractive feature. The
graceful, triple-arched loggia or
sala terrena, built to a plan of G
Pieroni in 1623–7, is approached
by an avenue of statues by the
Dutch sculptor Adrian de Vries –
they are copies, the originals
having been removed by the
Swedes during the Thirty Years
War. The ceiling is decorated
with paintings by B Bianco,
dating from 1629–30 – scenes,
appropriately enough, from the
Trojan Wars. A statue of
Hercules struggling with a
dragon presides over the large
pond, beyond which is the riding
school; this building is now used
as a branch of the National
Gallery.
Open: May to September, hours
vary.
Concerts are sometimes held in
the grounds.

NOVÉ MĚSTO

Nové Město or New Town forms the commercial and administrative centre of Prague; at its hub is Václavské náměstí (Wenceslas Square) (see p. 59). Despite its name the fortified settlement was actually founded in the Middle Ages. Nové Město was planned and built with great organisation: specifications were issued for the materials to be used, the height of the houses and the timing of their construction. Its concept was an outstanding feat of medieval town planning. The biggest of the towns of Prague, Nové Město's inhabitants were 'working class' and unsurprisingly it was a radical Hussite stronghold during the Revolution. Attempts to link the old and new towns were made repeatedly in the 14th, 15th and 16th centuries but none were successful until much later when in 1784 it became one of Prague's quarters. The area was cleared in the late 19th century and massive redevelopment took place. Today modern buildings stand together with many fine examples of the architectural styles employed since the beginning of the redevelopment.

Wenceslas Square is a long wide street rather than a square, lined with hotels and shops. It is Prague's main thoroughfare and social centre; a favourite haunt of locals and visitors alike. Originally a market place, the square was redesigned as a city boulevard in the mid-19th

More street than square, Václavské náměstí leads to Národní muzeum

century. Today the boulevard has a central avenue of grassy areas giving it an almost park-like appearance. Dominated by the monumental neo-Renaissance **Národní muzeum** (National Museum) Wenceslas Square has played an important part in most of Prague's major political upheavals. From the Hussite revolution to the demonstrations by the Civil Rights Movement which took place in the 1980s it has been an arena for political rallies.

◆
CHRÁM PANNY MARIE SNĚŽNÉ
(OUR LADY OF THE SNOWS)
Jungmannovo náměstí
This imposing Gothic church (the largest in Prague) was founded by Charles IV in 1347 but never completed. Its history is inextricably linked with that of the Hussite movement. In 1419 the radical priest, Jan Želivský, a regular preacher at the church, led an attack on the New Town Hall in the course of which several of the King's councillors were hurled from the windows – an incident known as the First Defenestration of Prague. Three years later the councillors had their revenge when Želivský was burnt at the stake for heresy. The interior is a curious blend of Gothic, Renaissance and baroque styles. The painting of the Annunciation over the High Altar is by V V Reiner (1724). Since the 17th century the church has belonged to the Franciscan Order which is why the neighbouring restaurant is called U františkánů (presently closed for repairs).

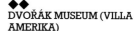

DVOŘÁK MUSEUM (VILLA AMERIKA)
Ke Karlovu 20
Metro: I P Pavlova
This beautiful baroque residence, built by Kilian Dientzenhofer in 1717–20, is known as the Villa Amerika after a 19th-century eating-house; a happy coincidence, as Dvořák's best known composition is his symphony *To the New World*. The exhibits include manuscripts, photographs, personal effects and correspondence with friends like the composer Johannes Brahms, and the conductor Hans von Bülow.
Open: Tuesday to Sunday 10.00 to 17.00 hrs.
Closed: Monday.

◆◆
KARLOVO NÁMĚSTÍ (CHARLES SQUARE)
Trams: 3, 4, 6, 16, 18, 21, 22, 24
The present park-like appearance of the largest square in Prague, dates from the mid-19th century. In medieval times, it was a market place and the hub of Nové Město, as we are reminded by the presence of the **Novoměstká radnice** (New Town Hall) at the northern end of the square. This grey, stone building with its typical Gothic tower, dates from the 15th century, although it has undergone a number of facelifts and reconstructions over the years. In 1419 it was the scene of the First Defenestration of Prague, when the rebel Hussite leader Jan Želivský unceremoniously evicted a number of government officials

Dvořák Museum, Villa Amerika

through a window on the premises.

Directly opposite, on the south side of the square, is the so-called **Faust House**. This attractive Renaissance building was given its baroque façade in the mid-18th century. Its chance occupation by two chemists, the Englishman Edward Kelly in the 16th century and the Czech Ferdinand Mladota, in the 18th gave rise to a supposed association with the legendary Dr Faustus. Kelly, already deprived of his ears after a conviction for fraud, disappointed the Emperor Rudolph II by failing to discover the Philosopher's Stone and, as a result, ended his days locked up in gaol.

Dominating the eastern side of the square is the **Jesuit College** and the **Church of St Ignatius**. Erected in 1665–70.

MUZEUM SNB A VOJSK MV (NATIONAL SECURITY CORPS MUSEUM)
Ke Karlovu 453,
Metro: I P Pavlova;
Bus: 252

How the Security Corps and the troops of the Interior Ministry prevented wayward Czech citizens from leaving the country in the 'good old days' before the Velvet Revolution. Fully illustrated!

Open: Tuesday to Sunday 10.00 to 17.00 hrs.
Closed: Monday and throughout July and August.

◆◆
NA PŘÍKOPĚ (ON THE MOAT)
This busy, pedestrianised shopping street takes its name from the moat which once formed a boundary between the Old and New Towns at this point. It's a useful place to change money: there are banks at

nos 14, 20 and 28; or you can go to the Čedote office at no. 18. The International Bookstore is opposite the Aeroflot offices at no. 20. There is an AGFA one-hour photo developing service at no. 17 and a jewellers (as well as glass and porcelain shops) in the arcade at no. 12. If you are hungry, there are several places to eat, including the Moskva Restaurant on the first floor of no. 29 and the Arbat burger bar on the ground floor. No. 15 is the children's department store, Dětský dům. Most of the buildings in the street are modern, for example the ČKD Engineering Works at no. 1. One notable exception is the baroque Sylva-Taroucca Palace, designed in 1743 by Kilian Dietzenhofer. The upper end of the street leads, via 28 října and the **Chrám Panny Marie Sněžné** (Church of Our Lady of the Snows), to Národni and the National Theatre. The lower part of Na Příkopé leads directly to Staré Mesto (The Old Town) and Prašna bránca Powder Tower and is also handy for the Týl Theatre and the Carolinum and is only a short walk away from the Obecní dům (Municipal House).

◆◆
NÁRODNÍ DIVADLO (NATIONAL THEATRE)
Narodní třída
Trams: 9, 17, 18, 21, 22
This striking cultural monument, in neo-Renaissance style, occupies a prime site overlooking the River Vltava. The foundation stones of the National Theatre were laid, with much pomp and ceremony, in 1868; included among them were stones from places which had played a leading role in the history of Bohemia and Moravia. Unhappily on 12 August 1881, soon after the theatre was completed, it was destroyed by fire. However tragedy turned into triumph when, partly funded by contributions from the public, a second National Theatre was rebuilt within two years.

In November 1883 the new theatre opened with the splendid premiere of Bedřich Smetana's opera *Libuše*. This second building was designed by Josef Schulz who incorporated the neighbouring Provisionary Theatre and a house into the complex. All the leading artists of the day contributed to its decoration. Just over a decade ago, between 1977 and 1983 this majestic building underwent extensive renovation and reconstruction. Its lavish decoration both inside and out was cleaned up and restored; new rooms were added and the staging equipment was modernised. Thus today's visitor has the same opportunity to appreciate this splendid building as those who visited it over a century ago.

It isn't only the interior that is worth a look. The loggia facing Národní has five arcades decorated with lunette paintings by Josef Tulka whilst on its attic floor there are statues of Apollo and Nine Muses by Bohuslav Schnirch. The latter was also the artist of the sculptural decoration on the frieze of the Loggia and statues on the northern façade. A sculpture modelled on Schnirch's work but which is in

Built at the height of the national revival, Národní Divadlo is the principal Czech theatre. Its interior decoration is superb

fact a later copy by Rous, Halman and Saloun can be seen on the main façade.
Anton Wagner sculpted the

NOVÉ MĚSTO

Národní Divadlo

statues of Záboj and Lumír which stand in niches on the north façade whilst on the western façade the work of Josef Myslbek can be seen. Myslbek is well represented inside the theatre too; it was he who sculpted the bronze busts of Smetana and Kolár in the portrait gallery (represented in the gallery are figures who have made an outstanding contribution to Czech dramatic art and opera) and at the front of the main foyer is his allegorical bronze statue *Music* dating from 1912. A series of 14 lunette paintings by Mikolas Aleš on the theme of 'My Country' and wall paintings also by Aleš and František Ženíšek are displayed in the large foyer of the first balcony. The paintings in the ante hall of the main foyer are by Adolf Liebscher.

Schnirch's work makes another appearance in the auditorium; with his sculptural group in the centre of the proscenium. Decorating the ceiling are eight fine allegorical paintings, again by Ženíšek while the origins of the National Theatre are illustrated in a detailed painting on the stage curtain by Vojtěch Hynais. Other work by Hynais in the theatre includes the frieze on the staircase to the presidential box; the paintings of the four seasons in the ladies' boudoir of the presidential box and the painting of St Cecilia in the Directors' reception room. Elsewhere are wall paintings celebrating the history of the Czech lands, important towns in Bohemia and Moravia and in the picture gallery, a series of paintings of the aforementioned towns, cities and regions which contributed to the foundations of the Theatre. This last series was painted in 1952.

The contemporary buildings which now form a closed square around the historic theatre are also part of the complex. They were built between 1977 and 1983 and designed by the architect K Prager and are connected with the old theatre by means of an underground tunnel. One is called The New Stage and features some of the most up-to-date theatre technology available.

The National Theatre is the principal Czech Theatre, the seat of an historic artistic culture. From its inception it has attracted many of the world's greatest performers and leading works from both the Czech and world repertoire have been performed here.

Interior, Národní muzeum

NÁRODNÍ MUZEUM
(NATIONAL MUSEUM)
Vítězného února 74,
Metro: Muzeum
Large helpings of natural history,
archaeology, palaeontology and
prehistory are served up in the
stolid, overblown building with
the gilded dome which presides
over Wenceslas Square. Not for
the casual visitor.
Open: Monday and Friday 09.00
to 16.00 hrs; Wednesday,
Thursday, Saturday and Sunday
09.00 to 17.00 hrs.
Closed: Tuesday.

◆◆◆
VÁCLAVSKÉ NÁMĚSTÍ
(WENCESLAS SQUARE)
Metro: Muzeum or Můstek
The heart of modern Prague,
Wenceslas Square is really a
stately boulevard, running on a
gentle downward slope from the

Národní Muzeum (National
Museum) at one end to the
fashionable shopping street
called Na přikopě at the other. In
the reign of Charles IV this area
was a horse market; until the end
of the 19th century, it was lined
with two and three-storey
baroque houses of the kind you
see elsewhere in the city. Little
of this survives and the only
architecture worth remarking on
is 20th-century.

For three dramatic weeks in
November and December 1989,
Wenceslas Square became the
focal point of resistance to the
long-discredited Communist
government. The events which
led to its overthrow, culminating
in a peaceful demonstration of
150,000 people amassed in front
of the National Museum, has
entered history as the Velvet
Revolution. Immediately
afterwards the imposing, but
ponderous, **statue of St
Wenceslas** served as a mixture

Jan Palach's protest is now openly remembered in Václavské náměstí

of national shrine and democracy wall, its steps strewn with flowers, lamps, images of the secular saints and heroes, flysheets and protest leaflets. A little further on, a second, smaller shrine has survived. This is dedicated to the memory of the Czech student, Jan Palach, who set fire to himself in protest against the Soviet invasion of August 1968.

Now that happier times have returned, Wenceslas Square has resumed its original role as a vibrant centre of commerce, entertainment and nightlife. Both sides of the street are lined with hotels, restaurants, cafés, shops, banks, tourist offices and night clubs. It is worth exploring the shopping arcades which date from the 1920s and 30s – for example, the **Lucerna** and **Alfa** (incidentally, a good example of

1920s constructivist architecture). Now rather gloomy and run down, they provide some insight into the drab side of life under Communism. In the cinemas up-to-date films can be seen and even a *comedy* about Karl Marx. Of the restaurants in the Square, the best known belong to the Ambassador and Zlatá Husa hotels (nos 5 and 7 respectively). Cabarets, floor shows and late-night discos are also on offer in these large entertainment complexes. More authentically Czech night-spots are to be found on the opposite side of the street and in nearby side-streets like Jungmannova. These vie with the ever growing number of strip-joints in the vicinity. Western newspapers and magazines are on sale from stands at the bottom of the Square and in nearby bookshops, such as Knihy Melantrich.

STARÉ MĚSTO

Over the river from Malá Strana, is Staré Město (the Old Town). During the reign of King Václav (Wenceslas) the settlement of merchants and craftsmen which had grown up across the river from Prague Castle was fortified and officially became a town in its own right. Not surprisingly it grew rapidly during the reign of the Přemyslid dynasty when Prague was among the most prominent towns in central Europe and later when it was the capital of the Holy Roman Empire.

Staré Město was the most important of the towns of Prague and consequently of the kingdom of Bohemia. Its prominent role is reflected in its architecture and the visitor will see a plethora of styles, many of them outstanding examples of their period. In 1893 part of the Staré Město was cleared and replaced with tenement houses. Happily though the rest of this splendid settlement was preserved and was officially deemed an Historical Reserve in 1971.

The town grew up around the **Staroměstské náměstí** (Old Town Square); its most famous attraction, the astronomical clock on the **Staroměstká radnice** (Old Town Hall). The assimilation of diverse architectural styles is illustrated here better than from anywhere else in the city. For example the baroque elegance of **Kostel svatého Mikuláše** (St Nicholas's Church) in one corner which strangely complements the gaunt angularity of the church of **Panny Maria před**

Týnem (Our Lady before Týn) situated in another. Adjoining streets are a further testimony to Prague's glorious past: a maze of half-concealed courtyards and alleyways, of convents and churches, theatres and taverns, shops and houses, each with its distinctive look and story.

Elsewhere in the Staré Město is the **Anežský klášter** (Convent of the Blessed Agnes), an important Early Gothic monument embracing in its history a good deal of the city's formidable past. Among numerous other notable buildings are the reconstructed 14th-century **Betlémska kaple** (Bethlehem Chapel) where Jan Hus taught and preached and which became an important centre of the Reformation movement; the art nouveau **Obecni dům** (Municipal Hall) which houses the Smetana Concert Hall and nearby, a Prague landmark, the **Prašna brána** (Powder Tower) forming an impressive entrance to the Staré Město.

Adjacent to the Staré Město is **Josefov** (The Jewish Town). Jews settled in Prague as early as the 10th century and their first communities were in Malá Strana. In 1986 much of the Jewish quarter which had grown up around the **Staronová synagóga** (Old-New Synagogue) was demolished. Major sights here are the Old-New Synagogue itself, the **Židovská radnice** (Jewish Town Hall) and the **Starý židovský hřbitov** (Old Jewish Cemetery). The area is also the location of the **Muzeum Umélecko-Průmyslové** (Museum of Decorative Art) which houses an important collection of glass.

◆◆◆
ANEŽSKY KLÁŠTER (ST AGNES CONVENT)

Anežská ulice
Buses: 125, 133, 144, 156, 187
Trams: 3, 26, 29

One of the oldest monuments in Prague and a national treasure, St Agnes' Convent is also a branch of the National Gallery. It is situated close to the Ultava River but public access is Via Anežká was founded in 1233 by the sister of King Václav (Wenceslas) I, Anežka (Agnes) of Bohemia. She introduced the Order of the Poor Clares (the female branch of the Franciscan Order) into Bohemia and became the abbess of the newly built convent in 1235. The medieval complex of buildings, consisting of two churches, several chapels, a cloister, the convent and a Minorite monastery was completed by the end of the 14th century.

*Anežsky klášter's **Gothic serenity***

During the Hussite Revolution the convent was deserted; the Dominicans occupied it again from 1556 to 1626 after which the Poor Clares returned. In 1782 the convent was dissolved. It was later abandoned, allowed to fall into ruin but in the late 19th century efforts were made to restore the neglected buildings, skillfully incorporating the surviving elements of the medieval structure. In particular the Chapel of St Saviour has been superbly restored and is an important example of the Bohemian Early Gothic style. During the reconstruction the burial places of members of the Přemyslid dynasty were unearthed, including the tombs of King Wenceslas I and Agnes of Bohemia; the tombs and artefacts found during the archaeological research are displayed in St Saviour's Chapel and the quadrangle of the Minorite monastery. The former chapel of St Francis has been

converted into a concert and lecture hall.

The cloister now houses the Museum of Applied Art including a display of glass from the kingdom of Bohemia, and a collection of paintings from the National Gallery. The gallery is devoted to Czech painting from the 18th and 19th century, mainly landscapes and portraits. The work of the leading artist of the period, Josef Mánes, is well represented; other artists include Karel Postl (1769–1818), Antonin Machek (1775–1844), Josef Navrátil (1796–1865) and Julius Mařák (1832–1899). Books and posters are on sale by the entrance, although they are predominantly in Czech. If you are now suffering from museum fatigue, this museum has its own restaurant, U Anežky, serving snacks as well as main meals.
Open: Daily 10.00 to 18.00 hrs.
Closed: Monday.

◆◆
BEDŘICH SMETANA MUSEUM
Novotného lávka 1
Trams: 17, 18
An exhibition documenting the tragic life of this great 19th-century Czech composer who ended his days in an asylum. The museum is located on a peninsula on the Smetana Embankment and is housed in the former municipal waterworks down by the Charles Bridge. On the façade there is a graffito decoration showing the battle with the Swedes on Charles Bridge in 1648.
Open: Wednesday to Monday 10.00 to 14.00 hrs.
Closed: Tuesday.

◆◆◆
BETLÉMSKÉ NÁMĚSTÍ (BETHLEHEM CHAPEL AND SQUARE)
Metro: Staroměstská, Můstek
Trams: 9, 17, 18, 21, 22
This quaint little section of old Prague is often missed by visitors – a pity. The large double-roofed building bearing more than a passing resemblance to a medieval manor house is in fact the Bethlehem Chapel. Unfortunately, owing to countless reconstructions, precious little of the original 14th-century hall survives. Yet the building is of great historical importance and was at the centre of the Reformation Movement.

From 1402 to 1413 Jan Hus preached at the Bethlehem Chapel, attracting a large number of people who came to listen to his provocative and ultimately heretical sermons criticizing the current social conditions and denouncing the Church establishment. The chapel's symbolic significance was recognized by another religious rebel, the German Thomas Münzer who chose to preach here a century later than Hus in 1521 – the same year that Luther was condemned at the Council of Worms. Münzer went on to lead a peasant's revolt against the German princes and was executed for his pains.

From 1609 to 1620 the chapel belonged to the Union of Czech Brethren; it then passed into the hands of the Jesuits and remained under their ownership until the Order was abolished in 1773. Most of the chapel was then demolished and a large dwelling house was built within the confines of the remaining walls.

In 1949 the house too was demolished and as, thirty years earlier, a preserved part of the chapel had been unearthed, archaeological research was set in motion and revealed that enough of the chapel had survived to enable the building to be reconstructed. This is what the visitor sees today.

The wooden parts of the chapel – the oratory, the choir and the pulpit – have been rebuilt and pupils of the Academy of Fine Arts were commissioned to decorate the walls with paintings illustrating the Jena Codex, Richenthal's Chronicle and the Velislav Bible. The remainders of tracts written by Jan Hus are also on display in the chapel. Adjoining the chapel on its eastern side is the preacher's house where Jan Hus lived and worked. Exhibits pertaining to his life and work and to the architectural development of the chapel are displayed here.

Open: Daily, April to September 09.00 to 18.00 hrs, October 09.00 to 17.00 hrs.

Closed: November to March.

Opposite the chapel is one of Prague's more stylish restaurants, U Plebána. A short walk from Bethlehem Square, on the corner of Karolíny Světlé and Konviktská, is the ancient **Kaple svatého Kříže** (Rotunda of the Holy Rood). This unusual Romanesque chapel dates from the early 12th century. Fragments of Gothic wall paintings are preserved in the nave.

The **Podebrad Palace**, situated to the rear of the Bethlehem Chapel on Řetězová 3, includes an excellently preserved Romanesque cellar which, unusually, is open to the public. It was built at the end of the 12th century for the Lords of Poděbrady, a powerful family which included a future King of Bohemia, George Poděbrady (1420–71).

Open: May to September, Tuesday to Sunday 10.00–18.00 hrs.

Closed: Monday and October to April.

◆◆◆
CELETNÁ
Metro: Staroměstská, Můstek
One of the oldest streets in Prague, Celetná takes its name from the bakers who sold their wares here in the Middle Ages. Its appearance today is mainly baroque, though vestiges of its medieval past remain. The east end of Celetná is dominated by the Prašná brána (Powder Tower). The building with the wrought iron balcony and classical statues (no. 36) is the former mint. It operated as a mint from the 16th century until 1783. Later commandeered by the Austrians, it was the scene, in 1848, of the initial clash between the citizens of Prague and the troops of General Windischgrätz. The ochre building, on the next corner, is Dům U Černé Matky boži (House At the Black Mother of God, no. 34) designed by the Cubist architect, J Gočár in 1911–12. Off to the right, down the side-street called U obecního domu, is the recently restored Hotel Paříž. It was built

just a few years earlier in the rival Art Nouveau style. The Dům U zlatého supa (House at the Golden Vulture, no. 22) stands on the site of a medieval brewery and is now the restaurant U Supa. The Buquoy Palace (no. 20) is named after Count Karel Buquoy, a distinguished general of the Thirty Years War. The present building dates from 1762 and belongs to the university. The Menhart House at no. 17 is now the restaurant U pavouka (At the Spider). The 18th century Hrzán Palace is at no. 12. Opposite, at

Prague is a city of surprises. In the baroque elegance of Celetná the house at the Black Mother of God has an uncompromising modern façade

no. 11, is the U zlatého jelena (At the Golden Stag). The medieval banqueting hall still functions as one of Prague's best known restaurants. Almost in the shadow of the Týn Church is the presbytery (no. 5) and, at no. 3, Dům U Tří králů (House At the Three Magi). This fine example of Gothic building, with its striking roof gables, dates from the 14th century.

◆◆◆
JOSEFOV

Jächymova
Metro: Staroměstská, Můstek
Buses: 133, 144, 156, 197
Tram: 17

The old Jewish quarter of Prague is situated just to the north of the Staré Město and can be approached directly from the street called Pařížská třída (Paris Avenue). The Jews moved here from Vyšehrad and the Malá Strana in the 13th century, following a decree of the 3rd Lateran Council that all Jews live within the confines of a walled ghetto. Most of the surviving buildings and monuments date from the 16th and 17th centuries, a period of unparalleled prosperity for the community. The area takes its present name from the Emperor Josef II, in whose reign the residence restrictions for Jews were abolished.

On the corner of Maiselova and Červená is the oldest surviving synagogue in Europe, the perversely named **Staronová synagóga** (Old-New Synagogue). Originally it was known as the 'New' or 'Great' synagogue but gained its present ambiguous name after another synagogue was built in the Jewish quarter in the 16th century. Staronová's well preserved Gothic interior dates from the 13th century and is its oldest surviving part. Unique in Bohemian architecture is the five-ribbed vaulting in the main hall; the motif used in the decoration and carving throughout is the number twelve to represent the twelve tribes of Israel. In the centre of the nave,

enclosed behind a late 15th-century iron grille, is the *almemor* or pulpit. A Torah shrine on the eastern wall contains a parchment scroll with the text of the Pentateuch (the five books of Moses and books 1–5 of the Bible).

To recognise the Jewish community's contribution during the Thirty Years War, in 1648 the Emperor Ferdinand presented the large flag displayed in the synagogue. The red flag with its star and cap has been used as the official banner of the Jews of Prague since it was presented. The capital is the only city in the world to carry the Jewish colours in its coat of arms.

The women's gallery was added in the 17th and 18th centuries and the exterior brick gables date from the 15th century. Directly opposite is the **Vysoká synagóga** (High Synagogue). This Renaissance building dates from 1568 and was originally part of the Jewish Town Hall. It is now a museum of arts and crafts. The textiles on display include richly embroidered Torah mantles, temple curtains, pulpit covers and vestments, mostly dating from the 18th century onwards, and there are some beautifully fashioned metal articles – candelabras, Torah shields, Hannukah lamps, goblets and spice containers among them. The pink and white building with the distinctive green steeple is the **Židovska radnice** (Jewish Town Hall), its 16th-century origins obscured by the baroque facelift it was given in 1765. Note the Hebrew clock, set in a gable beneath the tower. Its hands travel anti-clockwise, following the Hebrew lettering which is read from right to left.

The **Starý Židovsky hřbitov** (Old Jewish Cemetery) occupies a secluded site to the left of U Starého Hřbitova. One of Prague's most unusual monuments, its 12,000 tombstones sprout obliquely from the earth like so many broken and decaying teeth. The cemetery was used for burials from the mid-15th century until 1787, when the gates finally closed. The total number of graves is unknown but possibly exceeds 20,000 – a density which accounts for the uneven terrain. Many of the tombstones are decorated with reliefs, illustrating the name and occupation of the deceased (medical instruments, tailor's scissors, and so on). The distinguished scholar and rabbi Jehuda Löw (d 1609), credited by Jewish folklore with the creation of a Golen or robot, is buried here but you will need a guide to point out the grave. The oldest surviving tombstone belongs to the poet Avigdor Kara, and is dated 25 April 1439.

The **Klausova synagóga** (Klausen Synagogue) is also on U Starého Hřbitova, near the

The old Jewish Cemetery

entrance to the cemetery. A baroque building dating from the 17th century, it is now a museum exhibiting ancient Hebrew books and manuscripts. On the far side of the cemetery, in Široká Street, is the **Pinkasova synagógo** (Pinkas Synagogue), currently undergoing restoration. The original house incorporating the synagogue was built in 1535 by the wealthy Hořovský (Horowitz) family. It was enlarged and modified early in the 17th century, with the addition of a women's gallery, vestibule and assembly room. The building with the stone staircase at the top of U Starého Hřbitova is **Obradní síň** (Ceremonial Hall). The exhibition inside deals with that most harrowing episode in Jewish history, the Holocaust. During the Nazi occupation of 1939–45, 77,297 Jews, or 90 per cent of those in the ghetto, were slaughtered in the concentration camps of Bohemia and Moravia! The largest of the camps, Terezín (Theresienstadt), is the focus of this poignant exhibition, which includes drawings, poems and school exercises left by some of the 15,000 child inmates, as well as the records of the adult prisoners – some fine paintings, sketches, diaries, even music, all illustrative of day-to-day life in the camp and a sombre but reassuring reminder that the human spirit cannot be stifled, even in the face of the most barbaric cruelty.
Open: April to October, Sunday to Friday 09.00 to 17.00 hrs; November to March, Sunday to Friday 09.00 to 16.30 hrs.
Closed: Saturday.

KAROLINUM (CAROLINUM)
Železná 9
Metro: Můstek
Situated on Železná or Iron Street, the Carolinum (Charles University) was founded by Charles IV in 1348 and is the oldest university in Central Europe. At its core is the Rotlev house, donated by Wenceslas IV in 1383 and reconstructed in baroque style in 1718 (the oriel window, which protrudes rather incongruously from the façade, is a lone reminder of its medieval origins).

KLEMENTINUM (CLEMENTINUM)
Namestí primátora dr V Vacka
Metro: Staroměstská
Buses: 144, 156, 187
Tram: 12, 17
This vast and somewhat austere religious compound can be approached either from Karlova or Kžižovnická. It spreads out over an area of five acres (two hectares) and after the castle is the biggest complex of buildings in Prague. Built by the Jesuits between 1653 and 1726 it required the destruction of more than three dozen houses, churches, gardens and a monastery in order to make way for it.
Aside from the college building, the Clementinum (its name is derived from the old Church of St Clement which used to occupy part of the site) complex includes the churches of St Clement (a baroque edifice dating from 1711 has replaced the old church of the same name) and St Salvator, a chapel

Baroque Hall, Klementinum

belonging to the Italian Community and an observatory. It is also the home of the State Library of Czechoslovakia with over five million volumes and countless precious manuscripts included in a growing collection. The highlights include a glorious library, known as the Baroque Hall, found in the oldest west wing of the college building on the first floor. It was designed in the first half of the 18th century by F M Kaňka; its vaulted ceiling and dome are decorated with a painting and frescos by J Hiebl. Unfortunately the hall is presently closed to the public. Hiebl's work can also be seen in another wing of the college, the Mathematics Hall where a collection of table clocks is displayed. The neighbouring Mozart Hall has a rococo flavour in its decoration and furnishings and a further example of rococo art can be found in the chapel at the end of the main staircase. Standing in the same courtyard as a monument to J Steepling, the astronomer who founded the observatory tower, is the Mirror Chapel, also designed by Kaňka in 1724.

KOSTEL A KLÁŠTER SVATÉHO JAKUBA (ST JAMES CHURCH AND MONASTERY)
Malá Štupartská
Metro: Můstek
Trams: 3, 5, 24, 26

Tucked behind the **Týn Church**, on Malá Štupartská, is another medieval foundation, the former Minorite friary of St James. The original Gothic church was destroyed by fire in 1689 and immediately rebuilt in the baroque style. The barrel-vaulted ceiling is decorated with frescos by F Voget. Above the high altar, and set within a lavish gilt frame, is a painting of the martyrdom of St James by V V Reiner. On Sundays a choir and orchestra perform at the High Mass but there is much jockeying for position among the congregation.

◆◆
MUZEUM HLAVNÍHO MĚSTA PRAHY (CITY OF PRAGUE MUSEUM)

Sady Jana Švermy,
Metro: Florenc, formerly Sokolovská
Well-presented displays covering all aspects of the city's history. Period furniture, costumes, pottery, painted house signs, photographs, jewellery and much else besides. Everyone is impressed by A Langweil's vast model of the city dating from the 1820s and 1830s.
Open: Tuesday to Sunday 10.00 to 17.00 hrs.
Closed: Monday.

◆◆
MUZEUM UMĚLECKO-PRŮMYSLOVÉ (MUSEUM OF DECORATIVE ART)

Ulice 17 listopadu 2
Metro: Staroměstská

This fascinating exhibition of Czech crafts covers book-binding, glass making, clocks, pottery, furniture and porcelain, along with other fascinating exhibits.
Open: Tuesday to Sunday 09.00 to 12.00 hrs and 13.00 to 17.00 hrs.
Closed: Monday.

◆◆
OBECNÍ DŮM (THE MUNICIPAL HOUSE)

Náměstí republiky
In the 14th century King Wenceslas IV moved his court from Prague Castle to a palace he had built on the site now occupied by the Municipal House. It remained the seat of the Czech kings until late in the 15th century. A chequered history followed for this particular spot of the Staré

Obecní dům, a Czech extravaganza

Město; first there was a seminary on the site then, much later, a barracks and after that a school for cadets.

At the beginning of this century the place was cleared and between 1906 and 1912 the Municipal House was built. This extravagant monument to art nouveau was designed by Antonin Balšánek and Osvald Polívka. A host of artists contributed to both the exterior and interior decoration of the building although much of the ornamental decoration on the façade is the work of K Novák. Also on the façade is a mosaic entitled 'Homage to Prague' by K Špillar and a group of statues by L Šaloun. Figures wearing folk costume are shown in relief medallions on the sides of the building. The interior of the Municipal House is now a palatial community centre. At the centre of all this is the large **Smetana Concert Hall** decorated with sculptures by Novák and allegories of Czech dances by Šaloun. The wall paintings symbolising the dramatic arts are by Špillar. The Mayor's Hall is decorated with paintings by Alfons Mucha, an artist who designed a Pavilion for the Paris World Exhibition of 1900. Each room in the Municipal House has some kind of painting or adornment by leading artists of the time; The café even boasts a fountain, which was designed by J Pekárek.

The building has witnessed several scenes of importance in modern Czech history: the most momentous was the founding of the independent state of Czechoslovakia in October 1918.

POŠTOVNÍ MUZEUM (POSTAL MUSEUM)

Várů dům, Nové mlýny 2/1
Trams: 5, 24, 26
The history of Czech communications plus postage stamps from all over Europe.
Open: Tuesday to Sunday 09.00 to 17.00 hrs.
Closed: Monday.

PRAŠNÁ BRÁNA (THE POWDER TOWER)

Náměstí republiky
Metro: Můstek
Trams: 5, 10, 24, 26
The gateway to the Staré Město is the Powder Tower. Its name recalls a time in the 17th century when the tower was used for storing gunpowder but it actually dates from the late 15th century. Its function was purely ceremonial; the coronation procession began here before moving off towards St Vitus Cathedral. Originally the tower was left uncompleted when in 1484 the King moved his court from the neighbouring Royal Palace (see **Obecní dům**) back to Prague Castle. The tower was severely damaged during the Prussian siege of Prague in 1737 and although fragments of 15th-century sculptural decoration have been preserved, its present appearance owes much to the imagination of the 19th century architect J Mocker.
Open: Saturday, Sunday, Wednesday and public holidays, May to September 10.00 to 18.00 hrs; April and October 10.00 to 17.00 hrs.
Closed: Monday, Tuesday, Thursday, Friday.

◆◆◆ STAROMĚSTSKÉ NÁMĚSTÍ (OLD TOWN SQUARE)

Metro: Staromestská

In the Middle Ages, the vast open space now known as Old Town Square was a thriving market place, visited not only by the citizens of Prague but by traders from across Europe. Occupying centre stage is the dramatic statue of Jan Hus, erected in 1915 on the 500th anniversary of his execution for heresy. Today Staroměstské náměstí provides a colourful backdrop for circus, music and political theatre. The optimism is infectious – a far cry from the nightmare of August 1968, when the square reverberated with the drone of Soviet tanks crushing the life out of the 'Prague Spring'.

An enchanting medieval clock draws the crowds to a side wall of the **Staroměstská radnice** (Old Town Hall). Its delicately balanced mechanisms contrive to give not only the time of day but the months and seasons of the year, the signs of the zodiac, the course of the sun and moon and much else besides. On the stroke of the hour, death, in the form of a skeleton, tolls a bell before Christ and the twelve Apostles emerge in procession. A cock crows above their heads and the clock strikes.

The Town Hall itself is made up of four adjoining houses: Wölflin's House, granted to the burghers of the town by King John of Luxemburg and Bohemia in 1338, its superbly decorated portal windows framed by gilded escutcheons; the pink, Křiž House, purchased in 1360

and later embellished with a stunning Renaissance window, inscribed 'Praga caput regni'; the Mikeš's House and the house At the Cock (U kohouta), Romanesque in origin but with a much later façade. Adjoining this range of buildings is a later edition, the house At the Minute (U Minuty), distinguished by its sgraffito decoration with classical and biblical motifs.

The Old Town Hall is open to the public. In the vestibule, on the ground floor, there are substantial remains of the original Gothic arcades and vaulting. A staircase leads to the council chamber, known as the Hall of the Mayors of the City. This handsome room, with its fine casetto ceiling, dates from 1470 and was once part of Wölflin's House. The Gothic portals are copies. The adjoining chapel is the work of Peter Parler, who was also responsible for St Vitus Cathedral and the Charles Bridge. A nave with monumental walls and heavy ribbed vaulting leads, through a massive stone arch, to the presbyterium or sanctuary, which is decorated with frescos of heraldic designs, dating from

The astronomical clock at the Old Town Hall in Staroměstské náměstí is an around-the-clock attraction

the second half of the 14th-century. The portal bears the emblem of King Wenceslas IV – a textile ring with two kingfishers and the letter E (for Euphemia, his wife). An outstanding feature of the chapel is the modern stained-glass window, which bathes the floor and walls in a pool of coloured light. The Assembly Hall (1880) contains two paintings by the Czech artist, V Brožík – *Jan Hus before the Council of Constance* and *The Election of George of Poděbrady*. Another flight of steps provides access to the tower.

Opposite the entrance to the Old Town Hall, is a cluster of splendid baroque houses built on Gothic or Romanesque foundations: (l. to r.) no. 25 the Dům U modré hvězdy (house At the Blue Star) with the restaurant U bindrů (At the Binders); no. 26

house On the Stones; no. 27 (beyond the arches of Melantrichova) the house At the Ox; no. 28, formerly part of the Servite monastery; and no. 29, the house At the Golden Angel – note the oriel window, part of the original chapel. On the corner of Železná is the house At the Golden Unicorn (no. 20). Don't be fooled by the 18th-century fronting – the foundations of the

A medieval market place, Staroměstské náměstí still buzzes

building are 800 years old. The main portal, decorated with lilies, dates from the 15th century and there are many other surviving medieval features. The composer Smetana founded a music school here in 1848.

The grey stone towers and pinnacles of **Kostel Panny Marie před Týnem** (Church of Our Lady before Týn) dominate the eastern side of the Square (access through the archways of the Týn School). The present church was begun in 1365 and

was completed only in 1457. For much of the 15th and 16th centuries it was in the hands of the Hussites, religious nationalists condemned by the Catholic Church for their belief in the Utraquist heresy, that communion should be taken in both kinds. It was not until the Battle of the White Mountain in 1620 that the Protestants were finally defeated. The interior is an uneasy compromise of Gothic and baroque styles. Most of the painting is 17th century, but there is a medieval Pietà in a side chapel at the east end. The pulpit and the tin font are also 15th century. Distinguished astronomer Tycho Brahe (1546–1601) is buried on the right-hand side of the church in front of the high altar. The tomb bears his likeness in marble relief.

The houses occupying the eastern side of the square, and partly obscuring the Týn church from view, are also worth a closer look. The house At the White Unicorn (no. 15) has a cellar dating from the 12th century though its present appearance is 18th-century baroque. No. 14, with the lovely painting of the Virgin on the façade, is the Týn School. Also medieval in origin, it was reconstructed in the 16th century in the style of the Venetian Renaissance (note the gables). The dazzling house At the Stone Bell (no. 13) was remodelled by John of Luxemburg early in the 14th century. The recently restored Gothic façade preserves much of the original sculptural detail, including the exquisite window tracery. The house Sign of the Bell can be seen at the right-hand corner, below the pediment. The decorative flourishes of the **Golz-Kinský Palace** (no. 12) are rococo in inspiration and date from the mid-18th century. Nowadays the palace houses the National Gallery's collection of graphic art.

Kostel svatého Mikuláše (Church of St Nicholas), on the far side of the square, actually predates the Týn Church, although the present building is 18th-century baroque (1732–5). The elegant façade, with its sleek lines and fine proportions, implies a more ample interior than is in fact the case. Since 1920 the church has belonged to the Hussite Community. The novelist Franz Kafka was born next-door.

◆◆◆
TÝLOVO DIVADLO (TÝL THEATRE)

Metro: Můstek
Trams: 5, 9, 19, 29
Situated in Železná, alongside the **Karolinum**, is the neoclassical Týl Theatre, built in 1781–3. Originally known as the Nostitz Theatre after its founder, Count Nostitz-Reineck, the world premiere of Mozart's opera *Don Giovanni* was staged here on 29 October 1787. Another distinguished composer, Carlo Maria von Weber, was musical director of the theatre from 1813 to 1816. In 1945 it was rechristened after the 19th-century Czech dramatist Josef Týl. The theatre has been restored and there has been no public access for some years. However, it is due to be re-opened in the early 1990s.

STARÉ MĚSTO

UHELNÝ TRH

An area of charming old houses
and winding streets, connected
by gated courtyards. There was
a medieval coal market in
Uhelný trh which gives it its
name. The site of the colliers'
workshop is now occupied by an
18th-century fountain. Its
bacchanalian decoration makes
happy but unwitting reference to
the wine bars which give the
area its present character. Beer
enthusiasts take heart – one of
the best bars in Prague, U Dvou
Koček, is at no. 10. There is a
great deal of essential
restoration work currently going
on in Michalská.

The house At the Iron Door is
Early Gothic (13th century) with
Renaissance additions – note the
portal and gables facing Jilská.
Drink has been sold on the
premises since the 16th century;
formerly an ale house, it is now a
wine bar. U Vejvodů on Jilská
(no. 4) is another well-known
tavern, unbeatable for its beery,
bustling atmosphere. It takes its
full name from its 18th-century
owner, Jan Vejvoda of
Stromberg, whose coat-of-arms
you are able to see over the
portal.

Many of the period houses in
Melantrichova are now shops:
souvenirs are sold at no. 9 and
dolls and toys at Igrá, near no. 17.
The Barberina wine bar is at
no. 7.

The monastery and church of St
Michael (no. 17) is undergoing
restoration. If you are lucky, you
may be able to see traces of the
original Gothic fabric emerging
from beneath the 18th-century
plaster work.

VYŠEHRAD
Metro: Vyšehrad
The station used to be named
after Klement Gottwald, the first
Communist President of
Czechoslovakia. The popular
choice for a new name would
have been Civic Forum, but the
authorities settled on Vyšehrad.
Towering over the station is one
of Prague's newest hotels, the
Forum. The modernistic building
on the far side of the flyover is
the **Palace of Culture**, built in
1981, a multi-purpose complex
used primarily for concerts and
conferences.

There was a castle in Vyšehrad
as early as the 11th century
which, for a short while, was the
royal seat of the Přemyslid
dynasty. By the late Middle
Ages, however, the area had
become something of a
backwater and it never revived
in importance. The main points
of interest are down by the river,
near the neo-Gothic, twin-spired
Church of SS Peter and Paul.
Dating from the 19th century, it
conceals a number of earlier
buildings on the same site, the
remains of which are now being
uncovered by archaeologists.
There is a 14th-century painting
of the Virgin in the church.
Among the notables buried in
the cemetery next door are the
composers Antonín Dvořak and
Bedřich Smetana, the artist
Alfons Mucha and the writer
Karel Čapek.

Just a stone's throw away is the
Romanesque **St Martin's
Rotunda**, founded in the 11th
century and one of the earliest
Christian monuments in
Czechoslovakia.

IN THE SUBURBS

◆◆◆
BERTRAMKA (MOZART MUSEUM)

Mozartova 169, Praha 5
Tram: 4, 7, 9

The Villa Bertramka lies among the greener fringes of the industrial suburb of Smíchov; Mozart stayed here on his frequent visits to Prague as the guest of the Dušek family. It was here also that he completed, at a furious speed, the opera *Don Giovanni* which received its first performance in the Týl Theatre in 1787. Legend has it that the last notes of the work were written in the garden. The museum faithfully recreates the villa as it would have appeared in the composer's own day and the 18th-century furnishings include the harpsichord and

Mozart Museum, Villa Bertramka

piano on which he actually played.

Open: April–September, Tuesday–Fri 14.00–17.00 hrs; Saturday, Sunday 10.00–12.00 hrs and 14.00–17.00 hrs; October–March, Tuesday–Friday 13.00–16.00 hrs; Saturday, Sunday 10.00–12.00 hrs; 14.00–16.00 hrs.

◆◆
COLLECTION OF MODERN ART

Trade Fair Pavillion, Julius Fučík Park, Praha 7
Currently being reorganised.

◆◆
NÁRODNÍ TECHNICKÉ MUZEUM (NATIONAL TECHNICAL MUSEUM)

Kostelní 42, Praha 7
Trams: 1, 8, 25, 26

Well worth a visit, despite being rather remotely situated in the northern suburb of Holešovice. A wide-ranging display of

machinery and technical instruments, including the car in which the Archduke Franz Ferdinand was assassinated in June 1914 and astronomical instruments used by the 17th-century scientist Johannes Kepler. Television, radio, air transport and the cinema are all represented.
Open: Tuesday to Sunday 09.00 to 17.00 hrs.
Closed: Monday.

OUTSIDE PRAGUE

◆◆
KARLOVY VARY
By train: Rail services are infrequent and unduly prolonged. Take the bus!
By bus: Regular service from Florenc station (*Metro: Florenc*). Approximate journey time – 3 hours.
By road: Highway 6, west Prague.

Charles IV is said to have put Karlovy Vary on the map by accidentally discovering the thermal springs when one of his hunting dogs was scalded by a jet of hot water. However, it was not until the 19th century that the town, then known as Karlsbad, became established as one of Europe's most fashionable resorts. Goethe came here, so did Bismarck, Karl Marx, Alexander II of Russia, Brahms, Liszt and many other celebrities. Karlovy Vary is situated in a narrow, wooded valley. The best way to enjoy the town is to amble through the colonnaded streets and gardens, drinking in the genteel atmosphere. The spa water can be tasted at the fountains on the Yuri Gagarin

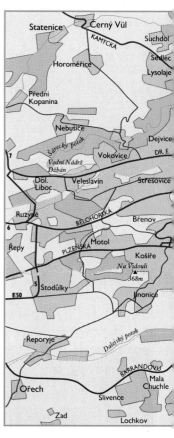

Colonnade; you can shop for Bohemian crystal, produced at the local **Moser Glassworks** or, if the town is too sedate for you, you can always explore the surrounding hillside. There are plenty of places to eat and drink. The best restaurants are in the hotels, especially the **Central** (with live music for dancing) and the **Moskva**. Nightlife too centres on the hotels and you can get a late night drink in most of them.

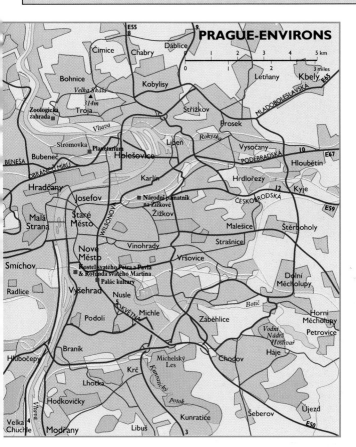

PRAGUE-ENVIRONS

Don't leave Karlovy Vary without sampling the local home grown liqueur – Becherovka. If you wish to stay overnight, you will need to make a reservation in advance, especially in the summer – Čedok will be able to help with this.

The Čedok office is at Trziste 23 (tel: 27798). Call in here for information about theatre, concerts and the biennial international film festival.

◆◆
KARLŠTEJN

By train: There is a regular suburban rail service (trains approximately hourly) from Smíchov station – *Metro: Smíchovské nádraží.* Journey time 50 mins.

By road: Highway 4 or 5, south-west Prague.

Nestling in an attractive wooded landscape, the pretty village of Karlštejn is only about 17 miles

OUTSIDE PRAGUE

Karlštejn's royal castle

(28 km) from Prague and is an ideal day, or even half-day trip. The 14th-century Gothic castle dominates the hillside but, surprisingly, cannot be seen from the station. Turn right, then left across the river to reach the village. The castle is directly ahead. The village is geared to cater for tourists in the summer and there are plenty of restaurants, souvenir shops and other facilities. There is a homely atmosphere in the **Restaurace u koronu**, though it is difficult to make yourself understood in English.

The castle was built in 1348–57 to guard the Imperial treasures, including the crown jewels, and to house Charles IV's impressive collection of relics. The Emperor's taste for meditation was as pronounced as his passion for hunting and Karlštejn provided plenty of opportunity to indulge in both. In 1422 the castle sustained a seige by

Hussite forces, lasting for seven months. Badly damaged during the Thirty Years War, it declined in importance thereafter. Its excellent state of preservation is due partly to a major restoration undertaken towards the end of the 19th century. The castle interior is open to the public. The Chapel of the Holy Rood, inside the main keep, dates from 1360. Sumptuously decorated throughout, its walls are inlaid with more than 2,000 semi-precious stones. The painted wood panels of the saints by Master Theodoric are copies – the originals can be seen in the National Gallery. The Chapel of St Catherine, in the smaller tower, was the Emperor's private oratory where he was not to be disturbed – important messages were relayed through a slit in the wall. Next door is the Church of Our Lady, with a fine timber ceiling and exquisite medieval wall paintings, the earliest of which dates from the 14th century.

Extensive restoration work is being undertaken at the moment, so parts of the castle may be closed.

Open: Tuesday to Sunday, May to September 08.00 to 18.00 hrs; March, April and October to December 09.00 to 16.00 hrs. *Closed:* Monday and all of January and February.

◆
KONOPIŠTĚ

By bus: from Florenc station (*Metro: Florenc*), then a short walk to the castle.
By car: take the E55, leaving south of Prague.
By train: express train to

Benešov then local bus to the castle.

The chateau at Konopiště served as a hunting lodge for successive Austrian Emperors and Archdukes – Kaiser Wilhelm II also stayed here. It once belonged to the heir to the Habsburg throne, the Archduke Franz Ferdinand, whose assassination on 28 June 1914 led to the outbreak of the World War I. The castle is built on medieval foundations but its present appearance is largely 19th century. The landscaped park is pleasant to stroll in but the central attraction is the exhibition of hunting paraphernalia including armour and weapons dating back to the 16th century.

Open: Tuesday to Sunday, May to August 09.00 to 18.00 hrs; September 09.00 to 17.00 hrs; April and October 09.00 to 16.00 hrs.
Closed: Monday and all of November to March.

◆
KUTNÁ HORA

By train: From Praha Holešovice (*Metro: Nádraži Holešovice*).
By car: Highway 12, leaving east of Prague.

Kutná Hora lies about 40 miles (65 km) south-east of Prague. The discovery of large deposits of silver ore in the 13th century turned it overnight into one of the boom towns of Central Europe. The mint, founded in 1300, continued to produce Bohemian

St Barbara's Cathedral, Kutná Hora

groschen until 1547. By the 18th century however the mines were exhausted and the town fell into decline.

Kutná Hora's medieval prosperity is attested to by its rich architectural heritage. The **Cathedral of St Barbara** (the patron saint of miners) is a monument to the ingenuity of Peter Parler's team of architects, who began work on the building in 1388 – it was completed in 1565. Look out for the magnificent vaulted roof and the medieval frescos. At the far end of Barborská is the **Hrádek**, originally part of the town's defences. The interior is now a museum of mining and minting. The tall spire rising above Havlíčkovo náměstí belongs to the Church of St James (14th century). Also in the square is the original mint, known as the Italian Court. (Italian bankers financed the mines.) Both the chapel and tower date from the 13th century and are open to the public – the interior decoration is worth seeing. A short stroll through the town to náměstí 1 máje leads to **Kamenný dùm** (The Stone House) with its remarkable oriel windows and decorated façade.

Information Office: Palackého náměstí.

EXCURSIONS-PEACE AND QUIET

PEACE AND QUIET

Wildlife and Countryside in and around Prague

by Paul Sterry

Fortunately for those seeking relaxation and wildlife interest, there are parks and gardens close to the centre of Prague, while for the more adventurous, national parks, reserves and areas of natural beauty can be found within reasonable driving distances.

Czechoslovakia is an elongated country, roughly 450 miles (724 km) long and 150 miles (241 km) wide. It comprises three regions: Bohemia in the west, Moravia in the centre and Slovakia in the east. The southwest, bordering Austria and Hungary, is generally flat, the land being an extension of the Great Hungarian Plain. Not surprisingly, much of it is now agricultural, while to the west, industry has made its mark. Slovakia, the eastern region of the country, has been least affected by man. A high proportion of this region is wooded.

Peace and Quiet in Prague

There are a substantial number of green parks and gardens

European lynx

within Prague, and pleasant strolls can be had along the winding course of the Vltava. The following parks are particularly worth visiting: **Stromovka Park** lies close to the banks of the Vltava, with parking available off U Sjezdoveho Palace in Holešovice. Avoid the eastern end of the park – the Julius Fučik Park of Culture and Recreation – if you want to watch birds. Look for woodpeckers, finches and, during the summer months, collared and red-breasted flycatchers. These latter two species catch insects using regular perches as lookout posts. Collared flycatchers have largely black-and-white plumage, while red-breasted flycatchers have an orange-buff breast and white patches at the base of the tail.

The woods around **Prague Castle** or **Hradčany** also provide good opportunities for watching birds. The castle can be reached from Obránců Míru or on tram 22. The nearest metro is Malostranská.

For a relaxing stroll, visit the Franciscan Gardens on the south side of the Church of St Mary of

the Snows at Jungmannovo
náměstí in Staré Město; the
nearest metro is Můstek.
The Botanic Gardens at Ulice Na
slupi in Nové Město are well
worth visiting for their displays of
native and introduced species.

Wildlife of Woods and Forests

Czechoslovakia's forests are
very varied in nature. The lowest
hills are usually covered in
beech and maple, with pines
appearing with increasing
elevation; spruce dominates the
higher levels right up to the tree
line. With such variety in
composition, it is not surprising
that the wildlife is also varied.
In spring, flowers such as violets
and primroses appear on the
woodland floor, followed by a
succession of orchids; the latter
do particularly well on areas of
limestone. Butterflies are also a
conspicuous feature of woodland
rides and glades, with fritillaries
and Camberwell beautys being
especially prominent. Fritillaries
are orange-brown with dark-
spots and Camberwell beautys
are maroon with a cream border.
The woodlands are especially
good for birdwatching. Several
species of tits and finches are
resident, as are nuthatches and
treecreepers. Woodpeckers
also live in the forests. The
largest is the black woodpecker,
which has all-dark plumage (the
crown is red in males).
Woodland mammals are
generally much more secretive
than the birds and are
consequently often difficult to
see. Brown bears are now
extremely rare, but martens, red
squirrels, wild cats and roe deer
are more widespread.

The lizard orchid

Wildlife of Lakes and Freshwater

Czechoslovakia has many lakes
and wetlands, especially in the
low-lying south of the country.
Many of these are rich in
freshwater life and support a
wide variety of birds.
In the spring, the margins of
many lakes are enlivened by the
colourful flowers of emergent
plants. Frogs and toads provide
a chorus of song to attract mates,
and spawning shoals of fish can
be seen in the lakes and river
backwaters. Herons, egrets and
grebes thrive on this bonanza,
while other species depend on
plant or insect life for their diet.
Several species of warblers can
be found in the reed-beds and
marshy scrub around many

PEACE AND QUIET

Wall lizards can be seen basking on rocks in the karst country

ponds and lakes. Most are rather similar in appearance and so their songs are the best clues to their identities. Savi's warblers have a reeling, almost mechanical song rather like a distant sewing machine, while river warblers utter a repetitive chirp very similar to the song of the field crickets that abound in Czechoslovakia's undisturbed meadows.

Karst Country
Many parts of Czechoslovakia to the south of Prague comprise limestone bedrock. Over time, mildly acidic rainwater has eroded strange shapes in the rock. Above the ground there are gorges, pillars and sinkholes, while below are extensive caves; this landscape is known as *karst*. One of the most accessible areas of karst is the Bohemian karst, southwest of Prague; explore the area between Beroun (on the E12) and the castle at Karlštejn.

Wall Lizard
Wall lizards reach the north of their range in Czechoslovakia. The pattern on the back of these long, slender animals is rather variable, but is a variation of grey or brown with darker streaks. Breeding males usually have orange underparts. In karst country, they sunbathe on rock faces, but they are wary and retreat to the safety of a crevice if disturbed.

Krkonoše National Park (Mountains of the Giants)

This area of wooded mountains lies northeast of Prague on the Polish border and can be reached by driving on the E14 from the capital. There are chair lifts and numerous trails and paths, the best known of which is the ridge trail running from Harrachov to Snezha along the border. The park's administrative centre is at Vrchlabi, which is a good base from which to explore the area. The forests are good for woodland birds; above the treeline, species such as Alpine accentors can be found. These little birds, about 7 inches (18 cm) long, have mottled brown plumage over a grey background. Though not notably colourful or exciting in their habits they are among the mountain birds that birdwatchers are especially keen to see.

Jeseník Mountains

This mountain range lies east of the Krkonoše Mountains on the Polish border, and is reached by driving east to Hradec Králové and then northeast to Jeseník or Sumperk. There are marked paths and a road climbs almost to the summit of the highest peak, Praded. The forest here is largely unspoilt – beech, pine or spruce according to elevation – and there are also upland lakes and extensive areas above the treeline.

Novozámecký rybnik (New Castle Pond)

Lying near Česka Lípa, north of Prague, this is a pond and wetland reserve. To reach it,

The Nutcracker

As its name suggests, the nutcracker feeds primarily on seeds and nuts, its preference being for hazel nuts. This elegant member of the crow family has brown plumage speckled with white and a white tail with a black band. In flight, it can be recognised by its rounded wings and short tail. Outside the breeding season, nutcrackers are usually seen in small flocks, feeding either in trees or on the ground; they are sometimes very approachable. They are common in upland areas of woodland in Czechoslovakia.

drive north via Mělník and explore the wetlands to the south of the city along the way. Black-headed gulls have a large breeding colony in the area. Also look for red-crested pochards, males of which have an orange head and red bill.

Lednicke rybniky (Lednice Ponds)

This series of ponds and surrounding wetlands lie close to the Austrian border southeast of Prague. Take the E15 out of the capital towards Brno. From here, head south to Mikulov and then take the road to Břeclav; at Lednice explore the ponds to the southwest using minor roads. Look for herons, white storks and numerous warblers. Black kites are common and can be told by their dark plumage and forked tail, which is flexed in flight.

Třeboň

Třeboň is at the heart of another wetland area almost due south of Prague, close to the border with Austria. To reach it drive south

PEACE AND QUIET

on the E14 via Tábor; the best areas of ponds lie between Veselí n Luž and Třeboň either side of the road. Many of the ponds are used to rear carp; some are now reserves. Birds of prey, herons and storks thrive on the abundant freshwater life.

The Danube

Between Bratislava and Komárno the Danube divides into two rivers. The land between the Danube proper and the Little Danube is effectively an island criss-crossed by a network of marshes, agricultural land and drainage channels.

This gentle landscape continues north of the rivers as far as Trnava and is dotted with lakes and marshes. Wetland birds are here in abundance and the area is the best in Czechoslovakia for great bustards. These immense but shy birds – males are Europe's heaviest birds – are becoming increasingly rare as the open habitat they require becomes fragmented and disturbed. They are sometimes seen in flight, when they resemble huge geese with black and white on the wings.

Hiking in Low Tatra Mountains

Penduline tit

> ### Penduline Tit
> The willows and poplars fringing many of the marshes and drainage channels along the course of the Danube provide ideal habitats for one of Czechoslovakia's most engaging birds, the penduline tit. Acrobatic and lively, they are often seen feeding in small flocks, in trees. Their chestnut backs, grey heads and conspicuous black face 'masks' make them easy to identify. In the breeding season they build elaborate, woven nests suspended from the end of a branch.

The Šumava Hills
Cloaked in the Bohemian Forest, this is one of the most unspoilt areas of woodland in Czechoslovakia. It lies along the German border and is the watershed of the River Vltava. The administrative centre is in Sušice, which can be reached by heading southwest from Prague on the road to Příbram but continuing south to Strakonice. From there continue northwest to Horažd'ovice and southwest to Sušice. A road runs south from Sušice along the valley of the Vydra and is extremely scenic. Czechoslovakia's largest reservoir – Lipenská – also lies in these hills.

The Tatra Mountains
These mountains dominate eastern Czechoslovakia and run along the Polish border. Much of the area is protected by national park status, the headquarters of which are at Tartranská Lomnica. The slopes are wooded with beech, pine and spruce, although much of the

PEACE AND QUIET

Female Ural owl

area actually lies above the
treeline.
Woodpeckers, capercaillies and
other birds are likely to be seen
in the woods, and if you are very
lucky you might see one of the
few European brown bears that
remain here. Above the forests,
chamois might be seen on rocky
crags, along with Alpine
accentors and ring ouzels. This
large area is a popular tourist
destination and information
about walks and trails can be
obtained fairly easily in most
towns.

The Vratna Valley
This beautiful wooded valley lies
in the Mala Fatra (Little Fatra
Mountains) in eastern
Czechoslovakia. To reach it from
Prague, travel southeast to
Olomouc and take the E7 to
Hranice and then the E85 to
Žilina. Shortly after the town,
take the road northeast to
Terchová; the Vratna valley lies

south of Terchova. The
woodland wildlife includes
bears, red deer, capercaillies
and woodpeckers, while above
the tree line look for alpine
flowers and golden eagles.

The Ural Owl
The Tatra Mountains are one of
the European strongholds for the
Ural owl, which only lives on
forested slopes. It is a large bird
– 24 inches (60 cms) in length –
with broad, rounded wings and a
comparatively long tail. Its
plumage is brown; there are
darker streaks on the breast and
the face is unmarked. Although
they feed mainly at night, Ural
owls are sometimes seen
perched on branches during the
daytime. If you happen to be near
a nest – usually built in a hollow
tree – they can be extremely
aggressive and will attack if you
do not leave. After dark, their
deep 'hoo-hoo-hoo' call carries a
long distance on still nights.

FOOD AND DRINK

You need not fear going hungry in Czechoslovakia, as the national dishes are exceptionally rich and filling. They are also heavily meat-based, which is bad news for vegetarians. (One of the few restaurants in Prague to cater specifically for vegetarians is listed below.) Restaurants in the major hotels, of course, offer a wide range of dishes and you will find the food here more nutritious, with fresh salads and more fruit and vegetables than you're likely to encounter in the average Czech establishment. However, you will have to pay a lot more, too. Besides Czech and Slovak delicacies, you can sample Chinese, French, Italian, Russian and other dishes in the various national restaurants, although the quality won't always live up to what you might expect in the West. If you are not too partial to meat, there are a number of fish restaurants in Prague and we've included several in our list. Czech starters can be a meal in themselves. Prague ham (*pražská šunka*) is a local favourite, sometimes served with horseradish (*s křenem*) or pickle (*se okurkou*), or you might try mushrooms and eggs (*žampióny s vejci*). The soups (*polévky*) are tasty. We particularly recommend a vegetable soup called *kulajda* if it is on the menu; alternatively, try potato soup with mushrooms (*bramborová polévka s houbami*) – delicious! If you prefer a consommé, look out for *hnědá* or *hovězí*

Of the main courses, omelettes (*omeleta*) are a good bet, served

The Vepřové se zelím is on the good soldier Schweik

FOOD AND DRINK

Advertising the devil's brew

with sauerkraut (*vepřové se zelím*), roast loin of beef with cream sauce (*svíčková na smetaně*), steak and eggs (*biftek s vejcem*) and goulash (*guláš*). If you are eating in a fish restaurant, you might find boiled carp with melted butter (*kapr vařený s máslem*) on the menu. Alternatively, roast pike (*pečená štika*) or trout in melted butter (*pstruh na másle*). Main courses are generally served with potatoes (*brambory*) and you will probably feel the need for a salad (*salát*) of some kind. Bread is often available as a matter of course. Otherwise, ask for *chleba*.

For dessert – if you still have room – try apple strudel (*jablkový závin*), pancakes (*palačinky*), jam omelette (*omeleta se zavařeninou*) or plum dumplings (*švestkové knedlíky*). The ice-cream (*zmrzlína*) is also good. If you would rather end your meal with cheese, point to *sýry* on the menu.

usually with ham (*se šunkou*) or mushrooms (*se žampíony* or *houby*). Roast ham with asparagus (*zapečené šunka s chřestem*) is another menu regular. For something more substantial, breaded veal cutlet, known to the Austrians as 'Wiener schnitzel' and to the Czechs as *smažený řízek*, should fill you up, especially if you order dumplings (*knedlíky*) as a side dish. These appear in a variety of forms, sometimes rounded, sometimes sliced, sometimes flecked with bread or bacon – always fattening! Other standard main courses include roast pork

Beer and Wine

Czechoslovak beer is justly famous throughout the world for its taste and potency. The Bohemian town of Plzeň is the centre of the industry and the quality beer, Pilsner Urquell (*Plzeňský Prazdroj*) is widely available. Budweiser too, you may be surprised to learn originates in Czechoslovakia, where it is known as *Budvar* – it is very different from its American variant. The local brews are just as good: *Pragžanka*, for example, brewed in the suburb of Holešovice. If your preference is for dark beer,

FOOD AND DRINK

look out for *U Fleků* (there is a pub bearing that name in Prague). The strength of the beer (either 12 or 14 per cent) is usually indicated on the menu. The general word for beer is *pivo*.

The Czechs are less well known for their wines, introduced from Burgundy by the Emperor Charles IV in the 14th century. Nowadays, the best vintages hail from Moravia and Slovakia, although the Bohemian wines of the Mělník region also have a good reputation. You will find them on sale in most Prague wine bars. You will also find a wide range of wines from abroad, especially French and German. White wine is *víno bílé*, red wine, *víno červené*. There are three very different types of liqueur worth sampling. *Borovička* is fiery, in the way of an Italian *grappa*, and should be treated with the same respect. *Slivovice* is a very winning plum brandy but best of all is the wonderfully aromatic *becherovka*, a herb-based drink concocted in the spa town of Karlovy Vary.

By this stage of the proceedings, you'll be in need of a coffee (*káva*). If you don't ask specifically for an espresso, you are likely to be served Turkish coffee, which comes with the grounds included. Tea is *čaj*.

Eating Out

Eating out in Prague is still extremely good value – if you can find a table. Unfortunately, at the moment most restaurants outside the hotels are fully booked at weekends and often on weekdays as well. There is no easy solution to this problem, save to say that you should book as far ahead as possible. The alternative is to turn up on spec in the hope that a table becomes available. Don't necessarily be put off by the *reservé* sign at the door; a table *may* become available – consult the head waiter about your chances. As most Czechs tend to eat early (any time from 17.30 hours onwards), the best time to arrive, if you haven't booked, is probably about 19.30 to 20.00 hours. Hopefully the lifting of restrictions on private enterprise should lead to an improvement in the long run.

There are several different types of eating house: *restaurace*, usually found in hotels; *vinárny*, literally wine restaurants although they actually sell beer as well; *pivnice*, beer halls or pubs which also sell food, although in rather basic surroundings; and *kavárny*, corresponding to the English café. There are limited restrictions on smoking in restaurants although apparently none in pubs. Service is usually included but a tip of about 10 per cent is customary.

Restaurants

Bohemia, Panorama Hotel, Milevská 7, Praha 4 (tel: 41 61 11). Bohemian and Slovak cuisine at hotel prices.

Čínská Restaurace, Vodičkova 19, Praha 1 (tel: 26 26 97). Fashionable and pricey, specialising in Cantonese and Szechuan cuisine with Bohemian overtones!
Closed: Sundays.

Chodské Pohostinství, Újezd 5, Praha 5 (tel: 54 05 31).

FOOD AND DRINK

Specialities of the Chod region of western Czechoslovakia.

Francouzska, Obecní dům, náměstí Republiky, Praha 1 (tel: 231 06 16). The restaurant, serving French and Czech food in opulent surroundings, can be found to the right of the entrance hall.

Kosher Restaurant, Maiselova 18, Praha 1 (tel: 231 09 09). Located in the heart of the old Jewish quarter. *Open:* only for lunch, 11.30 to 13.30 hrs.

Moskva, Na příkopě 29, Praha 1 (tel: 26 58 21). A large, rather brash restaurant offering Georgian as well as Russian specialities.

Myslivna, Jagellonská 21, Praha 3 (tel: 27 74 16). A popular restaurant with an excellent line in venison and pheasant. Close to Flora metro station.

Staropražská Rychta, Ambassador Hotel, Václavské náměstí 5–7, Praha 1 (tel: 22 13 51). Czech cuisine in a simple setting. *Open:* daily, 11.30 to 23.00 hrs.

Thang Long, Šimáčkova 21, Praha 7, (tel: 806 51). Vietnamese cooking in the Holešovice district.

Valdštejnská hospoda, Valdštejnské náměstí 7, Malá Strana, Praha 1 (tel: 53 61 95). Bohemian cuisine in the noble surroundings of Wallenstein Square.

Vegetárka, Celetná 3, Praha 1 (tel: 232 46 05). One of the very few vegetarian restaurants in Prague and only a stone's throw from Old Town Square.

Vikárka, Vikárská 6, Hradčany, Praha 1 (tel: 53 51 58). In great demand because of its location inside Prague Castle and

opposite St Vitus Cathedral.

Viola Trattoria, Národní 7, Praha 1 (tel: 235 87 79). Fancy a break from Czech cuisine? This Italian restaurant is in the heart of the Staré Město, not far from the National Theatre.

Vltavská Rybí Restaurace, Podolská 2, Praha 4 (tel: 43 11 90). A fish restaurant in the Vyšehrad district.

Wine Restaurants

Bistro Non-stop, Slovanský dům, Na příkopě 24, Praha 1 (tel: 22 35 88). No-nonsense meals in a former neoclassical palace.

Lobkovická, Vlašská 17, Malá Strana, Praha 1 (tel: 51 01 85).

Eating out: the writing's on the wall

The former quarters of the Imperial Officer Corps. Authentic Czech cuisine and wines.

Na Baště, náměstí U sv. Jiří, Hradčany, Praha 1 (tel: 53 90 61). Garden restaurant within the Castle walls.

Opera-Grill, Divadelní 24, Praha 1 (tel: 26 55 08). Handy for the National Theatre.

Tři Grácie, Novotného lávka, Praha 1 (tel: 26 87 46). A charming restaurant in a delightful setting close to the Charles Bridge.

U Anežki, Areál Anežského kláštera 12, Praha 1 (tel: 231 00 84). A clean, simple eating house inside St Agnes Convent. Try 'The Monk's Pocket' – pork cutlet stuffed with cheese and spicey sausage. *Closed:* Monday.

U Golema, Maislova 8, Praha 1 (tel: 231 03 72). Čedok recommends this fish restaurant located in the heart of the Staré Město. *Closed:* Sunday.

U Malířů, Maltézské náměstí 11, Malá Strana, Praha 1 (tel: 53 18 83). 'The painters', a small but stylish restaurant near the church of the Maltese Knights. Quality wines.

U Plebána, Betlémské náměstí 10, Praha 1 (tel: 26 52 23). A warm

FOOD AND DRINK

intimate restaurant, hung with
17th-century engravings. Very
unplebeian, despite the name.
Choice of cuisines but the Czech
dishes, especially the *kulajda*
(vegetable) soup, can be
recommended.
U Prince, Staroměstské radnice,
Praha 1 (tel: 22 62 72). Down-to-
earth, friendly restaurant, much
patronised by Czechs.
U Zelené Lipy, Železná, Praha 1
(tel: 22 78 15). A new bar-
restaurant, favoured by the
young. Stylish ambience created
by design touches such as
plants, mirrors and spotlights.
Good, friendly service.
U Zlaté hrušky, Nový svět 3,
Praha 1 (tel: 53 11 33). A popular
restaurant in a picturesque area
of Hradčany.
Železné Dveře, Michalská 19,
Praha 1 (tel: 26 27 31). Actually in
a courtyard between Michalská
and Jilská. There has been a
wine tavern here since the 16th
century. Good food in a cosy
atmosphere, but the live musical
performances can be a
nuisance.
Znojemská, Hotel Ambassador,
Václavské náměstí 5–7, Praha 1
(tel: 214 31 20). Plain Czech fare
served up in an over-busy
atmosphere. Rather sullen
service.

Cafés

Arbat, Na příkopě 29, Praha 1
(tel: 26 58 21). Fast food with a
difference. This brightly-lit
burger-bar features Soviet
cuisine, including shashliks and
kebabs from the southern
republics.
American Hospitality Center, U
kapra, Malé náměstí 14, Praha 1.
A newcomer to the Prague

scene, the centre deals primarily
with information but popcorn
and soft drinks are also on sale
here.
Café de Colombia, Mostecká 1,
Malá Strana, Praha 1 (tel: 536 68
35).
Espresso, Nerudova 27, Malá
Strana, Praha 1.
Kavarna pasáž, Hotel Ambassador,
Václavské náměstí 5–7, Praha 1
(tel: 214 31 20).
Kavarna u Sixtu, Celetná, Praha 1.
Kavarna u Tyna, Staroměstské
náměstí, Praha 1.
Modrá čajouna, Jilská 16, Praha 1.
A tea house.
Savarin, Na příkopě 10, Praha 1
(tel: 22 05 66).
U Bindrů, Staroměstské náměstí,
Praha 1.
Ve Zlaté Uličce, Zlatá uličce,
Hradčany, Praha 1. A bistro in
the grounds of Prague Castle.

Beer Halls *(pivnice)*

U Bonaparta, Nerudova 29, Malá
Strana, Praha 1 (tel: 53 97 80).
U Černého Vola, Loretánské
náměstí 1, Praha (tel: 53 86 37).
U Dvou Koček, U Helný trh 10,
Praha 1 (tel: 26 77 29).
U Fleků, Křemencova 11, Praha 1
(tel: 29 24 36).
U Kalicha, Na Bojišti 12, Praha 2
(tel: 29 07 01).
U sv Tomáše, Letenská 12, Praha
1 (tel: 53 00 64).
U Supa, Celetná 22, Praha 1
(tel: 22 30 42).
**U Vejvodů, Jilská 4, Praha 1
(tel: 22 06 86).**
U Zlatého Tygra, Husova 17,
Praha 1 (tel: 26 52 19).

Book ahead if you plan to visit a
restaurant. If the place is full
when you arrive, however, it is
worthwhile waiting for a table.

SHOPPING

The glass counter at the Kotva state department store

Prague's pedestrianised streets and compact city centre make it a pleasant place to shop in, even if the stores themselves are nothing exceptional. You will find it interesting to visit one of the now old-fashioned state department stores – the best known are **Kotva** (the Anchor) and **Máj** (for addresses see below). The limited range and indifferent quality of the consumer goods on offer here will give you an insight into one of the reasons why the peoples of Eastern Europe are crying out for change.

Some ideas for presents include Bohemian glassware which is sure to please (look out especially for the Moser label). There are also attractive porcelain figurines, hand-carved puppets and embroidered tablecloths. *Becherovka*, a liqueur derived from herbs, *slivovice* (plum brandy) and the Slovak juniper brandy called *borovička* are robust liquid alternatives. If you want a lasting memento of your holiday, why not buy a recording of Czech folk music or of one of the great classical works by Smetana or Janáček (Smetana's *Ma Vlast*, for example, or Janáček's *Glagolithic Mass*)?

The shops are generally open from Monday to Friday 09.00 to 18.00 hours and Saturday 09.00 to 12.00 hours. Large department stores like Kotva and Máj stay open on Saturday afternoons. Most shops are closed on Sundays.

You can pick up cheap and cheerful mementos of your visit

SHOPPING

in the big department stores. Kotva, for example, sells football favours, T-shirts, badges, tea-towels etc. The following outlets sell a wider range of souvenirs:
Václavské náměstí 28, 47, Praha 1.
Celetná 1, Praha 1.
Malé náměstí 10, Praha 1.
Na můstku 1, Praha 1.
Tuzex stores sell Czech and imported goods of every description, payment for which is exclusively in hard currency. Purchases may be taken out of the country duty free so make sure all receipts are kept. Tuzex hard currency stores specialize in different goods. For instance clothes can be bought at **Benetton**, Revoluční 2, Praha 1; cameras at **Železná 18**, Praha 1; food and drink at **Náměstí Míru 3**, Praha 2; jewellery at **Rytířska 13**, Praha 1; cosmetics and perfumes at **Va**

smečkách 24, Praha 1; and car accessories at **Skořepka 4**, Praha 1.

Glass and Porcelain
Czechoslovakia is world famous for its crystal glassware and porcelain. The best outlets in Prague for these products are **Bohemia Moser**, Na příkopě 12, Praha 1, where some purchases are for hard currency only; **Diamant**, Václavské náměstí 3, Praha 1; **Crystalex**, Malé náměstí 6, Praha 1; **Krystal**, Celetná 20, Praha 1; and **Bohemia Glass**, Pařížská 2, Praha 1.
Other specialist shops include:

Jewellery
Bijoux de Boheme, Staroměstské náměstí 6, Praha 1.
Václavské náměstí 9, 53, Praha 1.
Národní 15, 23, 38, Praha 1.
Jindřišská 10, Praha 1.

Bold and effective—Civic Forum umbrellas in Czech colours

Antiques
Václavské náměstí 60, Praha 1.
Celetná 12, Praha 1.
Uhelný trh. 6, Praha 1.
Mikulandská 7, Praha 1.
Národní 22, Praha 1.

Art (Dílo Galleries)
Galerie Na Újezdě, Újezd 19, Praha 1. Open Tuesday to Sunday. Closed Monday.
Galerie Na Můstku, 28 října 16, Praha 1. *Open:* Tuesday to Sunday. *Closed:* Monday.
Galerie Karolina, Železná 6, Praha 1.

Clothing and department stores
Kotva, náměstí Republiky 8, Praha 1.
Máj, Národní 26, Praha 1.
Dům módy, Václavské náměstí 58, Praha 1.
Dětský dům, Na příkopě 15, Praha 1 (Children's).
Družba, Václavské náměstí 21, Praha 1.

Food
Dům potravin, Václavské náměstí 59, Praha 1.

Sports Equipment
Dům sportu, Jungmannova 28, Praha 1.
Malé náměstí 14, Praha 1 (angling).

Books
Knihkupectví Melantrich, Na příkopě 3–5, Praha 1.
Knihkupectví U zlatého klasu, Na příkopě 23, Praha 1.

Records
Jungmannova 20, Praha 1.
Václavské náměstí 17, 51, Praha 1.

Agfa one-hour film developing service
Na příkopě 19, Praha 1.

ACCOMMODATION

Understandably, the Czech tourist industry has found it difficult to cope with the unprecedented demand for hotel and other accommodation following the 'Velvet Revolution' of November 1989. Consequently, you will need to book well in advance of your trip to avoid disappointment.

All hotel bookings currently go through Čedok, Czechoslovak State Travel Bureau (see **Directory, Tourist Information**). Package tourists usually end up in one of the major hotels of the Interhotel group, for example the Forum, Intercontinental or Panorama. There are also a number of cheaper hotels which you can book either through Čedok or in person. Our selection, arranged alphabetically, covers the entire spectrum, from 5-star luxury hotels to basic bed and breakfast accommodation. We have also included motels and riverside botels, which tend to be in the middle of the price range with facilities approximating to 3-star.

Expensive Hotels
Alcron, Štěpánská 40, Praha 1 (tel: 235 92 16). 143 rooms. A luxury hotel, just off Wenceslas Square. Plzeň regional cuisine is served in the restaurant.
Ambassador, Václavské náměstí 5 Praha 1 (tel: 22 13 51). 114 rooms. Overlooking Wenceslas Square and incorporating a large entertainment complex.
Esplanade, Washingtonova 19, Praha 1 (tel: 22 25 52). 63 rooms. In a secluded location near the National Museum, this is one of

ACCOMMODATION

Forum Hotel—spectacularly modern

Prague's best hotels.

Forum, Kongresová ul. Praha 4 (tel: 42 21 11 or 41 01 11). 531 rooms. A modern international hotel with conference centre, beer and bowling bar, fitness centre, swimming pool and casino. Close to the Palace of Culture and the Vyšehrad metro.

Intercontinental, náměstí Curieových, Praha 1 (tel: 231 18 12). 394 rooms. Prague's premier luxury hotel with views across the river to Prague Castle. The facilities include a conference centre and sauna. There is also a top category restaurant on the top floor and a wine bar.

Jalta, Václavské náměstí 45, Praha 1 (tel: 26 55 49). 84 rooms. A small, sombre-looking hotel on Wenceslas Square but with

excellent accommodation in the luxury hotel class.

Olympik, Sokolovská 138, Praha 8 (tel: 82 85 41). 317 rooms. A modern hotel not far from the city centre. Wining and dining facilities are offered in the international cuisine restaurant. The nearest metro station is Florenc.

Palace, Panská 12, Praha 1 (tel: 26 83 41). Situated just behind Wenceslas Square, this recently restored hotel was once patronised by the European aristocracy.

Panorama, Milevská 7, Praha 4 (tel: 41 61 11). 432 rooms. A large, skyscraper hotel. Facilities include a swimming pool and a Čedok tourist office. The hotel is only 100 yards/ metres from Pankrác metro.

Parkhotel, Veletržní 20, Praha 7 (tel: 380 71 11). 234 rooms. A modern hotel on the left bank, near Vltavská metro.

Reasonable Hotels

Družba, Václavské náměstí 16, Praha 1 (tel: 24 06 07 or 235 12 32). A small, centrally situated hotel overlooking Wenceslas Square.

Evropa, Václavské náměstí 25, Praha 1 (tel: 236 52 74). 110 rooms. A turn-of-the-century building of considerable historic interest, which is currently undergoing restoration.

Juventus, Blanická 10, Praha 2 (tel: 25 51 51). A student hotel with single and double rooms close to the Náměstí Míru metro. It is small, so it is often full.

Lunik, Londýnská 50, Praha 2 (tel: 225 66 17). In a quiet location near the I P Pavlova metro.

Meteor, Hybernská 6, Praha 1 (tel: 22 92 41). In a central

Evropa Hotel, from a more elegant age

location near náměstí Republiky. Lenin's Bolsheviks once met on this street but nowadays the Czechs don't want to know. The hotel offers basic facilities with a restaurant.

Opera, Těšnov 13, Praha 1 (tel: 231 56 09). Basic facilities with restaurant. Situated next to a noisy main road near Florenc metro.

Paříž, U Obecního domu 1, Praha 1 (tel: 232 20 51). 86 rooms. The Paříž is in a picturesque location near the Powder Tower. The hotel has been recently renovated and has a large, much frequented restaurant overlooking the street.

Splendid, Ovenecká 33, Praha 7 (tel: 37 54 51). On the left bank, not far from Vltavská metro. The hotel is very good, but only offers basic facilities.

Zlatá Husa, Václavské náměstí 7, Praha 1 (tel: 214 31 11). 72 rooms. Busy hotel on Wenceslas Square. Facilities include an entertainments complex.

Motels

Club, 252 43 Průhonice (tel: 75 95 13). Situated on the main Prague-Brno road about 12 miles (15 km) from the city centre. The motel has a swimming pool, sauna and nightclub.

Stop, Plzeňská 215a, Praha 5 (tel: 52 11 98). This motel has a bar and a restaurant. The nearest metro is Anděl.

Botels

Admirál, Hořejší nábřeží, Praha 5 (tel: 54 86 85). Found on the left bank, near the Palackého bridge. The Admirál has a bar and restaurant. The nearest metro is Anděl.

Albatros, nábřeží L. Svobody, Praha 1 (tel: 23 16 99 6). More basic accommodation but also with its own bar and restaurant. Reached by trams 5, 24 or 26.

Racek, Dvorecká louka, Praha 4 (tel: 42 57 93). Reached by tram 21; bar and restaurant.

Private Accommodation

The arrival of private enterprise is making this an increasingly attractive option. There is plenty of choice with more and more Czechs anxious to cash in on the expanding tourist industry. Bear in mind that not all the accommodation on offer is centrally situated, although most is within easy reach of public transport. Prices compare very favourably with hotels – you can take the family for a week in Prague for not much more than the cost of a one-night stay in a luxury hotel.

Čedok has an accommodation bureau at Panská ul 5, Praha 1 (tel: 22 56 57 or 22 70 04). Open daily 09.00 to 17.00 hrs. You have to commit yourself to at least three nights if you want a private room.

Pragotour, U Obecního domu 23, Praha 1 (tel: 231 72 81) also offers private accommodation, not usually very centrally situated. Again, a three night commitment is required.

A newcomer on the scene is Top Tour. Contact: Emil Hansal, Rybná 3, 110 00 Praha 1 (tel: 232 10 77). (Fax (02) 23208 60). You are advised to Fax your requirements through direct. Czechbook Agency operates from England. Address: 52, St John's Park, London SE3 7JP (tel: 081 853 1168). Michal Kodicek and Agnes Ambrose are offering a wide range of private accommodation in Prague and throughout Czechoslovakia. There is great enthusiasm on the part of the hosts and many are willing to conduct sightseeing tours, obtain theatre and concert tickets, provide English-speaking guides and in some cases rent out cars or bikes. Some will even offer to drive you from the airport. A deposit of 40 per cent is required on booking, with the balance to be paid not less than eight weeks before your departure date. Clients are advised to make their own insurance arrangements.

CULTURE, ENTERTAINMENT, NIGHTLIFE

Culturally, Prague is one of the best provided capitals of Europe, serving up a rich and heady offering of grand opera, ballet, classical theatre, mime, chamber and symphony concerts, folk dancing, jazz and disco. And the venues too are magnificent, ranging from the ornate splendours of the National Theatre to the Gothic intimacy of St Agnes Convent.

Theatre and concert performances generally begin at 19.30 hrs, but check before you set out. The times of recitals and chamber concerts vary. You can hear operas by the great Czech composers, Smetana, Dvořák, Janáček and Martinů at the National Theare, side by side with masterpieces by Mozart, Verdi, Rossini and Puccini. Ballet and theatre performances also take place here but modern theatre has its own stage – the **Nová scéna** where comedies by playwright and now President Václav Havel, compete with classic productions of Chekhov, Strindberg and Čapek. The Czech Philharmonic Orchestra gives regular symphony concerts but if you prefer something on a smaller scale, look out for recitals by the Virtuosi di Praga or the Martinů Quartet. Internationally renowned soloists like James Galway also drop in from time to time, although it may be a while before Placido Domingo is in Prague again.

Jazz is very much the front runner where popular music is concerned – see the listings below for the leading clubs. Live rock is not yet widely available so you may have to settle for the latest disco sounds. Children in particular will love the mime and puppet theatres for which Prague is famous but the Magic Lantern is for everyone. A perfect marriage of technical wizardry and artistic imagination, each show contrives a delicate balance of mime, music, poetry and film to stunning effect.

You can book theatre tickets through Čedok, your hotel or the ticket agencies listed in the **Directory** under **Entertainment Information**.

Opera, Ballet and Theatre

Národní divadlo (National Theatre), Národní 2, Praha 1 (tel: 20 53 64).
Smetana Theatre, Vítězného února 8 (tel: 26 97 46).
Nová scéna, Národní 2, Praha 1 (tel: 26 00 33).
Týlovo divadlo (Týl Theatre), Železná 11, Praha 1 (tel: 22 32 95) (closed for major restoration).
Mime – **Braník Theatre**, Branická 63, Praha 4 (tel: 46 05 07).
Magic Lantern – Jungmannova 31, Praha 1 (tel: 26 00 33).
Laterna Magica, Národní třída 40, Praha 1
Puppets – **Spejbl and Hurvinek**, Římská 45, Praha 2 (tel: 25 16 66).
Říše loutek, Žatecká 1, Praha 1 (tel: 232 34 29).

The beat on the street: informal entertainment in the Hradčany area

NIGHTLIFE

Music
Symphony concerts are given regularly in:
Dvořák Hall, náměstí Krasnoarmejců, Praha 1 (tel: 231 91 64).
Smetana Hall, Obecní dům, náměstí Republiky 5, Praha 1 (tel: 232 58 58).
Palace of Culture, 5 května 65, Praha 4 (tel: 417 27 91).
Janáček Hall, Besední 3, Praha 1 (tel: 53 05 46).
Smaller scale concerts are held at:
Agnes-Areal, U milosrdných 17, Praha 1 (tel: 231 42 51).
Bazilika sv Jiří (St George's Basilica), Hradčany, Praha 1.
Dům U kamenného zvonu (House At The Stone Bell), Staroměstské náměstí 13, Praha 1.
The **International Prague Spring Music Festival**, is held annually from 12 May to 4 June. Apart from the venues already listed, concerts take place in historic churches and palace halls, including St Vitus, St James, St Nicholas, the Bertramka, the Martinic and Wallenstein Palaces and the Clementinum, as well as the terraces and gardens around Prague Castle.

Operetta and Musicals
Hudební divadlo v Karlině (Karlín Music Theatre), Křižíkova 10, Praha 8 (tel: 22 08 95).

Folk Music and Jazz
Concerts of folk music from different regions are held at the **Municipal Library**, Mariánské náměstí 1, Praha 1 (tel: 84 81 14 and 684 01 02). They generally begin at 20.00 hrs. Jazz is poular in Prague and there are several venues such as the **Press Jazz Club**, Pařížská 9, Praha 1.

The club is on the first floor of the Union of Journalists building and includes a bar. Entertainment is provided by home-grown bands and smaller ensembles playing most types of jazz. It is open Monday to Friday until 02.00 hrs. Jazz is played at **Reduta**, Národní 20, Praha 1 (tel: 20 38 25), from 21.30 to late. **Viola**, Národní 7, Praha 1 (tel: 235 87 89) is a wine bar with Jazz groups and occasional poetry readings.
Malostranská Beseda, Malostranské nàměstí, Praha 1 (tel: 53 04 82) is another venue.

Cinemas
There are at least half a dozen cinemas in the shopping arcades off Wenceslas Square (eg Alfa, Blaník, Lucerna). Some Western films are shown with subtitles but avoid those marked with a small square – they have been dubbed into Czech.

Nightlife
Prague has quite a lively night life. Foreign businessmen are catered for by major hotels like the **Forum, Panorama** and **Intercontinental** which provide the usual bland fare of cabaret, discothéques and floor shows, all at highly inflated prices. Tourists and well-heeled Czechs alike head for the **Zlatá Husa** and **Ambassador** hotels in Wenceslas Square which have Western-style night clubs with discos and 'video-club' shows. Drinks are expensive, although not admission charges. *Strictly no jeans or trainers.* You will find ordinary Czech youngsters patronising the less glitzy establishments across the road, or round the corner in Národní (**Adria's** for example). The custom

is to book tables in advance, although this is not strictly necessary. There is generally a notional admission charge, good music and a limited range of drinks. Bouncers clubs have been known to demand a bribe in hard currency. Don't bother, it's not worth it.

Adria, Národní třh 40, Praha 1. From 20.30–midnight. Discothéque.

Alfa, Václavské náměstí 28, Praha 1. Open daily 18.00–1.00 hrs. Café with dancing.

Alhambra, Ambassador Hotel, Václavské náměstí 5, Praha 1. Revues and variety shows.

Astra, Václavské náměstí 28, Praha 1
Open daily 19.00–02.00 hrs. Discothéque.

Barberina, Melantrichova 10, Praha 1. Open Monday to Saturday 20.00–04.00 hrs. Wine bar with music and dancing.

Lucerna Bar, Štěpánská 61, Praha 1. Open daily 20.00–03.00 hrs. Cabaret and dancing.

Video-Disco, Hotel Zlatá Husá, Václavské náměstí 7, Praha 1. Open daily 19.30–02.00 hrs.

Symphony in the sun

WEATHER AND WHEN TO GO

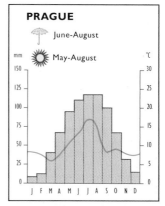

PRAGUE

☂ June-August

☀ May-August

Discothéque and floor show. Prague is a year-round destination. The climate is mild with an average yearly temperature of 48°F (9°C) so you won't need ski-boots or other outlandish gear! Summers are warm with a July average of 66°F (19°C) but expect some sharp frosts in December and January when temperatures often drop a few degrees below zero (January average 30°F −1°C). Expect a fair amount of rain throughout the year, especially in summer.

HOW TO BE A LOCAL

Czechs are a friendly, open people and you will find them very approachable. Obviously you will make more progress if you have at least a smattering of the language – even courtesy words like please, thank you, etc, can help break the ice. See **Language** page 125. Most Czechs understand German and an increasing number are coming to terms with English which has now replaced Russian as the compulsory foreign language in schools. If you are able to strike up a conversation, you will find out more about Prague in this way than you will ever learn from a guide book. Hotels tend to insulate foreigners from real life in the host country so spend as little time in this artificial atmosphere as possible. Better still, avoid hotels altogether and hire a private apartment for a week or two. It is much cheaper and you will get to meet more people in authentic Czech surroundings. (See **Accommodation** for details.) Eat out as much as possible but don't rely exclusively on the tried and tested recommendations of Čedok representatives. Look for places off the beaten track,

It's worth making the effort to get in touch with local life

where you are more likely to come across ordinary Czech people. The Czechs are great beer drinkers at any time of day and you will always find a welcome in the smoky but relaxed conviviality of a *pivnice*. Try the following, or any from the fuller list on page 96:
U Dvou Koček, U Helný trh 10, Praha 1.
U Fleků, Křemencova 11, Praha 1.
U Kalicha, Na Bojišti 12, Praha 2.
Locals make full use of the excellent public transport system and tend to leave their cars at home, so why not mix with the crowd? Or take one of the slow suburban trains from Smíchov station and have a leisurely look at the beautifully wooded countryside, typical of Bohemia. Take at least one taxi ride before you leave Prague. The drivers are as street-wise as anywhere and some speak good English. After five minutes in their company you will feel as if you have lived in Prague all your life.
Čedok organise evening parties for foreigners designed to provide a taste of Czech life. Attractions include brass band/dulcimer band in folk costumes, wining and dining on authentic Czech cuisine, wine-tasting competitions and folk dancing. 'Evening on the Vltava' allows you a romantic view of Prague at night from the deck of the Steamer *Vyšehrad* while eating Czech cakes and drinking your fill of local beer. All events are seasonal. Contact Čedok for details and advance ticket sales: Na příkopě 18, 111 35 Praha 1 (tel: 231 97 44).

CHILDREN

Taking children to Czechoslovakia presents no unusual problems. However, baby listening services are not widely available in hotels. Baby care items such as nappies, creams, tinned foods, etc, are readily available in department stores such as **Kotva** and there is a clothes store at **Dětský Dům**, Na příkopě 15, Praha 1.
Of the Prague sights, young children in particular will love the Old Town Hall with its performing clock as well as the view from the top. Horse-drawn carriages, known as *fiacres*, are available for hire in the Staroměstské náměstí (Old Town Square.) Prague Castle can be heavy going for youngsters, so it's a good idea to pause for the changing of the guard or to put your feet up for a few minutes in Zlatá ulička (Golden Lane). Not far from the Castle is the Petřín Park which has a maze, a hall of mirrors, a funicular railway and a smaller version of the Eiffel Tower (now a television tower) which offers excellent views from its upper gallery.
You may like to try a boat trip on the Vltava. The landing-stage is at the Rašínovo nábř, Praha 2 (tel: 29 38 03 and 29 83 09).
Prague Zoo is in the northern suburb of Troja, Praha 7, (tel: 84 14 41). (Take the metro to Nádraží Holešovice, then bus no. 112.) The natural woodland setting, overlooking the Vltava, makes for a pleasant and relaxed day out. Look out for the Przewalski horses, bred successfully here but now extinct in the wild. *Open:* daily

October to March 09.00 to 16.00 hrs; April 09.00 to 17.00 hrs; May 09.00 to 18.00 hrs; June to September 09.00 to 19.00 hrs.

The Observatory and Planetarium are at Petřín 205, Praha 1, (tel: 53 55 51/3) *Open:* daily throughout the year, performance times vary. *Closed:* Monday but it is open in the evenings.

Younger children will love a visit to the theatre. There are several to choose from, including the following:

Spejbl and Hurvinek Puppet Theatre, Římská 45, Praha 2 (tel: 25 16 66).

Říše loutek Puppet Theatre, Žatecká 1, Praha 1 (tel: 232 34 29).

Braník Mime Theatre, Branická 63, Praha 4 (tel: 46 05 07).

Magic Lantern Theatre Show, Národní třída 40, Praha 1 (tel: 26 00 33).

TIGHT BUDGET

Living in Prague is relatively cheap, though prices are likely to rise fairly steeply over the coming years. There are any number of cheap hotels in Prague, all of which provide basic facilities. However, Prague is a very popular town and budget hotels fill up quickly. You will have to book these independently through the following agencies:

Čedok, Panská ul. 5, Praha 1 (tel: 22 56 57/22 70 04). *Open:* daily 09.00 to 17.00 hrs.

Pragotour, U Obecního domu 23, Praha 1 (tel: 231 72 34/231 72 81). Pragotour also offers private accommodation. However, it is not usually very centrally situated and there is often a three night minimum stay.

Culture needn't be costly: art in action

Private agencies (new):
Top Tour, Emil Hansal, Rybná 3, 110 00 Praha 1 (tel: 232 10 77/232 08 60 or 229 65 26. Fax (02) 2320860). You are advised to Fax your requirements through direct.
Czechbook Agency, 52 St John's Park, London SE3 7JP (tel: (081) 853 1168).
A selection of cheaper hotels:
Juventus, Blanická 10, Praha 2 (tel: 25 51 51). Near Náměstí míru metro.
Lunik, Londýnská 50, Praha 2 (tel: 25 66 17). Near I P Pavlova metro.
Meteor, Hybernská 6, Praha 1 (tel: 22 92 41). Near náměstí Republiky.
Opera, Těšnov 13, Praha 1 (tel: 231 56 09). Near Florenc metro. If at all possible book in advance, otherwise you may have to queue. In the summer cheap accommodation is booked early in the day so try and organise this in the morning. If your accommodation is *very* basic it is useful to know that there are showers in the basement of the Hlavní nadraži station (Metro line C).
Public transport is extremely cheap and efficient both inside and outside Prague.
Dining out is still very good value, though you often have to queue for a table. Most beer bars (*pivnice*) serve acceptable and highly economical meals as well as drinks and you will enjoy the relaxed atmosphere. See **Food and Drink**. Or try the following cheap restaurants:
U Anežky, areál Anežského Kláštera 12, Praha 1 (tel: 231 42 51 ext. 35 (St Agnes Convent).
Staropražská Rychta,

(Ambassador Hotel) Václavské náměstí 7, Praha 1 (tel: 22 13 51).
Arbat, Na příkopě 29, Praha 1 (tel: 26 58 21) which serves fast food.
Entrance charges to museums and galleries are notional. Opera and theatre tickets are relatively expensive, though not by Western standards, but are also often difficult to get. Street musicians and dancers play regularly for free in the Old Town Square which is fine on warm summer nights. Hotel discothéques are expensive, but entrance to more homely Czech establishments like Adria's (see **Nightlife**) costs virtually nothing. There are also entertainers in many of the *pivnice*.
For cheap souvenirs, try shopping in a major department store like Kotva on Revoluční.

SPECIAL EVENTS

Spring/Summer

International Prague Spring Festival:
The annual International Prague Spring Music Festival begins on 12 May (the anniversary of Smetana's birth) and ends with a stirring performance of Beethoven's Ninth Symphony on 4 June. The main venue is Dvořák Hall but many of the concerts take place in historic churches and palace halls, some of which are rarely open to the public. Venues include St Vitus Cathedral, the churches of St James and St Nicholas, the Bertramka (Mozart museum), the Martinic and Wallenstein palaces, the Clementinum and the terraces and gardens which

are situated around Prague Castle.

Also held in June are **Concertino Praga**, when young performers are given the opportunity to demonstrate their skills, and **Golden Prague**, an international television festival.

Autumn/Winter
In October the **Prague International Jazz Festival** is held and, in February, the **Matthias Fair** takes place in Julius Fučik Park of Culture and Recreation in Holšovice.

Outside Prague
Other festivals in Czechoslovakia are located much further afield. They include: the biennial International Film Festival at Karlovy Vary (June); the Chod Region Folk Festival at Domažlice (south west of Plzeň) in August; the International Folklore Festival at Strážnice (between Brno and Bratislava) in June; the Bratislava Music Festival (September) and the Brno Music Festival (September).

SPORT AND LEISURE

Spectator Sports
Prague has two well-known football teams: Sparta ČKD (currently sponsored by Benetton) play at the stadium on Obránců míru 98, Letná, Praha 7, (tel: 38 24 41); Dukla play at Na Julisce, Dejvice, Praha 6 (tel: 32 51 40). The largest sports complex in the country, however, is in the suburb of Břevnov. It is one of the largest stadiums in the world and the huge, Communist-sponsored gymnastic displays known as Spartakiada used to take place here but are now a thing of the past. Čedok, or the *Month in Prague* will have information about all the sports on offer, including ice-hockey, volleyball, basketball and gymnastics. Czechoslovakia is famous for producing tennis stars of the calibre of Ivan Lendl and Martina Navratilova. Budding stars play on the practice courts at Štvanice Island, Holešovice, Praha 7, (tel: 231 63 23). There is horse racing at the State Course at Chuchle (tel: 543 541-2), about $7^{1}/_{2}$ miles (12 km) from the city centre. Take Metro Line B to Smíchovské nádraží, then bus no. 453.

Tickets and information available from:
SLUNA, Panská 4, Praha 1 (tel: 22 12 06).
ČSTV, Dukelských hrdinů 13, Praha 7 (tel: 37 58 49).

Other Sports
Swimming – Swimming in the River Vltava is not recommended. There are indoor swimming pools at Podolská 74, Podolí, Praha 4 (tel: 43 91 52);
Dům Kultury Klarov, Nábřeží kapitána Jaroše 3, Praha 1 (tel: 53 62 61);
Štvanice Island, Holešovice, Praha 7 (tel: 231 11 75).
There is open air swimming during the summer at Císařská Ionka (Císařský Island), Praha 5 (tel: 54 52 75); also on Štvanice Island, Holešovice, Praha 7.

Ice skating – There is an ice skating rink at the Štavnice Sports Complex, Štavnice Island, Praha 7.

Golf – There is a nine hole golf course situated at Motol, Praha 5.

DIRECTORY

Contents

Arriving

Passports and Visas

You need a passport valid for at least five months and although a Czech visa is *not* requiried by visitors from Canada, Eire, UK and US, they *are* required by visitors from Australia and New Zealand. The visa is valid for three months from the day of issue but may be extended with the help of Čedok. Transit visas are valid for 48 hours. Visas (not transit visas) may be issued on the spot at some border posts in special cases. Visa applications are available from Czechoslovak embassies:

Australia: Consulate General, 169 Military Road, Dover Heights, Sydney, NSW 2030 (tel: (02-371) 8878)

New Zealand: Czechoslovak Embassy, 12 Anne Street, Wadestown, PO Box 2843, Wellington (tel: (04) 723142).

Every visitor requiring visas *must* register with the police (hotels automatically do this for you). Registration office: Olsanska 2, Praha 3.

For transport queries contact these addresses:

Britain: Czechoslovak Embassy (visa section), 25 Kensington Palace Gardens, London W8 4QY (tel: (071) 229 1255)

Canada: Czechoslovak Embassy, 50 Rideau Terrace, Ottawa, Ontario, K1M 2A1 (tel: (613)749-4442)

US: Czechoslovak Embassy, 3900 Linnean Ave NW, Washington DC 20008 (tel: (202) 363-6319).

By Air

There are daily flights from London Heathrow (two hours) by British Airways or ČSA (Czechoslovak Airlines) and from New York by ČSA and Pan Am.

Ruzyně airport is about 12 miles (20 km) from Prague. Facilities at the moment are fairly primitive for an international airport, though there are some signs of renovation work. Caféterias, duty free shops, etc., are still very much on the Soviet model – ie poorly presented and stocked. Lounges too are sparsely furnished and there is little or no distinction between smoking and non-smoking. Fortunately, procedures are very straight-forward and there are unlikely to be delays. As well as handling international flights Ruzyně airport is a transit point for internal flights to Bratislava and Brno. Buses and taxis are available outside the airport to take you to the city centre. ČSA runs a half-hourly bus service until 19.00 hours from the airport to the Vltava terminal at Revoluční 25 and Čedok operate a bus to the main hotels four times a day.

Ruzyně Airport Central Information Service – tel: 36 77 60.

ČSA (Czechoslovak Airlines) offices:

Australia: Room 808/9 Australia Square Tower, Sydney 2000, NSW (tel: (02) 276196)
Britain: 72 Margaret Street, London W1N 7LF (tel: (071) 2551898)
Canada: 401 Bay Street, Suite 1510, Toronto M58 2Y4 (tel: (416) 363-3174)
USA: 545 Fifth Avenue, New York 10017 (tel: (212) 682-7541).

By Rail

Trains leave daily from London (Victoria) via Ostend and Germany. Or you can pick up a train in Vienna and Frankfurt. The journey from London to Prague is 30 hours. International trains arrive at **Hlavní nádraží** station in the centre of Prague. British Rail European Information Service – tel: (071) 834 2345. *NB* InterRail cards are valid for Czechoslovakia but Eurorail and other train cards are not. However an International Students Union Card (RUS) enables the bearer to have a 25 per cent reduction on fares in any Eastern bloc country.

By Car

Take the E-12 from Frankfurt to

Prague's pollution-free transport

Plzeň (border at Waidhaus-Rozvadov) or the E-15 from Berlin (border at Schmilka-Hřensko). Drivers must hold an international driving licence, the registration documents for the card and an international technical certificate and 'green card' (international insurance certificate). Petrol coupons are required for foreign cars so visitors *must* buy petrol vouchers (see **Motoring**).

Camping

Most campsites are open only between May and the beginning of October and can get very full in the summer. *Czechoslovakia Camping* is a guidebook listing A category campsites – *Autokempinky* (Motor camps) which have shower and toilet facilities and may sell food. The B category *Stanový tábor* are basic campsites with toilets. Some campsites have bungalows for hire as well. Neither bottled gas nor methylated spirit for cookers are readily available so take a supply with you.

For reservations contact the **Autoturist Organisation**, Na Rybníčku 16, Praha 2 (tel: 22 48 28)

Campsites around Prague
(A category with restaurants):
Caravan, Mladoboleslavská 72, Kbely, Praha 9 (tel: 89 25 32)
Caravancamp, Plzeňská, Praha 5 (tel: 52 47 14)
Kotva Bránik, (camping and bungalows) U ledáren 55, Praha 4 (tel: 46 13 97)
Na Vlachove, Rudé armády 217, Praha 8 (tel: 84 12 90)
Nedvězi, Nedvězi, Praha 10 (tel: 75 03 12)
Sportcamp, (camping and bungalows) V podháji, Praha 5

(tel: 52 18 02)
Transit, (bungalows B category) Ruzyně, 25. února 197, Praha 6 (at airport hotel, tel: 36 71 08).

Chemist (see **Pharmacist)**

Crime

Crime is very much on the increase in Prague, especially as more Western visitors flow to the city bringing with them valuable stocks of hard currency. So take all the normal precautions – watch out for pickpockets, use the hotel safe to store valuables and lock up your car. Changing money on the black market is a crime so avoid the temptation.
Police station, Konviktská 14, Praha 1 (tel: 21 21 11 11). In an emergency dial 158.

Customs Regulations

Customs regulations are strict. You will need a passport valid for at least another five months beyond the date of your visit as well as a visa where necessary (see **Arriving**).
No Czechoslovak currency may be brought in or out of the country; however, there are no restrictions on foreign currency.

Duty Free

Visitors may bring **in**:
2 litres of wine
1 litre of spirits
250 cigarettes *or* the equivalent in tobacco
$7\frac{1}{2}$ lbs (3 kg) food and gifts of a reasonable value. Of course drugs and firearms are illegal.
The following may be taken **out**:
2 litres of wine
1 litre of spirits
250 cigarettes *or* their equivalent small gifts and souvenirs
but not antiques, many foods, children's clothing, furs or

DIRECTORY

leather goods, gold and silver, unless purchased in **Tuzex** (duty-free, hard currency) shops. Keep all receipts for inspection.

Driving

The following papers are essential when motoring in Czechoslovakia and must be presented at the border: an international driving licence, car registration papers, green card insurance. You will also be expected to carry a nationality plate for your car, a first-aid kit and a red warning triangle to display in case you break down. Drive on the right.

Seat belts must be worn outside the cities and children under 12 are not allowed in the front seats. **Motorcyclists** must wear helmets and goggles.

Drinking and driving is absolutely forbidden and infringement carries heavy penalties. **All** accidents must be reported to the police.

Note: Wenceslas Square and Na příkopé are pedestrianised and permanently closed to traffic. Elsewhere there is little restricted access but bear in mind that Prague city centre is old with narrow, cobbled streets. Parking is prohibited in the central areas but spaces are available at major hotels, main line stations and also at the following metro stations: Dejvická, Hradčanska and Pankrác.

For motoring information on routes, road conditions, etc, contact: **Autoturist**, Central Office, Ječná 40, Praha 2 (tel: 29 09 56).

Speed Limits

Motorways 68 mph (110 kph),

motorcycles 49 mph (80 kph), major roads 56 mph (90 kph), motorcycles 49 mph (80 kph), built-up areas, all traffic 37 mph (60 kph).

Petrol Vouchers

Vouchers can be bought for hard currency at border crossing points or from the State Bank and travel offices.

In Britain petrol coupons are available in advance from Zivnostenska Bank, 18 King William Street, London EC4N 7BY (tel: (071) 283-3333). Diesel fuel (NAFTA) can be purchased only with special vouchers bought at any branch of the State Bank. Four gallons (20 litres) of fuel may be imported duty free.

NB Bear in mind that there is currently a severe fuel shortage throughout Czechoslovakia with queuing and some rationing. The situation is unlikely to improve in the forseeable future.

Petrol Stations

These are open from 06.00 to 20.00 hrs with a few 24-hour stations on the motorways and major roads into Prague. You may occasionally find unleaded petrol.

Emergency Breakdown Service

This is run by Autoturist's 'Yellow Angels', (tel: 154) or contract the garages at: Opletalova 21 (tel: 22 49 06) and at Limuzská 12, Praha 10 (tel: 77 34 55).

Garages can be found on the following streets (central Prague):

Svatoplukova, Praha 2
Olšanská, Praha 3
Újezd bei Průhonice, Praha 4
Argentinská, Praha 7
Spare parts are hard to get hold

Residents keeping time: a detail of the Astronomical Clock

of. Specialist garages can be found at:
Austin-Žižkov, Jeseniova 56, Praha 3 (tel: 27 23 20)
BMW—Severni XI Praha 4 (tel: 76 67 52)
Citroën—Za opravnou 1, Praha 5 (tel: 52 26 51)
Fiat—Na strži 35, Praha 4 (tel: 42 66 14)
Ford—Osiková 2, Praha 3 (tel: 82 95 00)
Renault—Ďáblicka 2, Praha 8 (tel: 88 78 03)
Volkswagen—Severni XI, Praha 4 (tel: 76 67 52).

Car Rental
Renting a car is very expensive and payment must be in hard currency or by credit card. You can drive into Czechoslovakia in a Western hire car (Hertz, Avis, etc; Hertz have an office in the Palace Hotel – see **Accommodation**, page 99) but, currently, the only Czech rental firm is **Pragocar**; Štěpánská 42 (tel: 235 28 25 or 235 28 09). (Available also at Prague airport and at international hotels.) Economy and luxury cars for a standard tariff per hour or day with unlimited mileage.

Electricity
220 volt 50 cycle AC. For shavers etc, take a standard continental adaptor with square pins. Visitors from the US or Canada with appliances normally requiring 100/120 volts and not fitted for dual voltage will need a voltage transformer.

Embassies and Consulates
Canada: Mickiewiczova 6, Praha 6

In Prague you can read the papers and go for a walk at the same time

(tel: 31 20 25 1–4)
UK: Thunovská 14, Praha 1
(tel: 53 33 47)
USA: Tržiště 15, Praha 1
(tel: 53 66 41).

Emergency Telephone Numbers
Ambulance 333
Doctor 155
Fire 150
Police 158

Entertainment Information
Tickets for theatre, concerts and
sports events can be obtained
from:
Prague Information Service,
Na příkopé 20, Praha 1
(tel: 54 44 44).
**House of Soviet Science and
Culture**, Rytířská 31, Praha 1.
SLUNA, Panská 4, Pasáž Černá
růže, Praha 1 (tel: 22 12 06).
SLUNA, Václavské náměstí 28,

Pasáž Alfa, Praha 1 (tel: 26 16 02).
AVE Ltd, Hlavní nádraží
Wilsonova 80, Praha 1 (tel: 236 25
60, 236 25 41 or 236 30 75).
Any of these agencies, as well as
Čedok and the information desks
at most hotels, will provide you
with a copy of the monthly
'what's on' leaflet: '*Prague
Cultural Events*'.
See also **Culture, Entertainment
and Nightlife**.

Entry Formalities (see Arriving)

Health Care
All emergency treatment is free
for foreign visitors and some
additional medical care is free
for British subjects only under an
agreement between the two
countries. There is a clinic for
foreigners at **Fakultni poliklinika**,
Karlovo náměstí 32, Praha 2,
(tel: 29 93 81 or 29 13 53).
Open: 08.00 to 16.15 hrs, or contact
your hotel desk for the address

117

of the local Outpatient
Department.
Emergency dental treatment is
available at **Vladislavova 22**,
Praha 1 (tel: 26 13 14). Evenings
and weekends. See also
**Emergency Telephone
Numbers**.
There are a number of health
spas in western Bohemia,
Karlovy Vary for example. For
information and booking consult
Čedok or contact Balnea,
Pařížská 11 Praha 1 (tel: 23 23 76
7, telex 0122215).
See also **Pharmacies**.

Lost Property

Main Office: Bolzanova 5, Praha 1
(tel: 24 84 30);
for documents: Olšanská 2, Praha
3, (tel: 24 51 84).

Media

Foreign language newspapers
are becoming ever more widely
available, especially in and
around Wenceslas Square.
English speakers can choose
from *The Guardian*, the *Financial
Times*, *The Economist*, *Time
Magazine*, the *International
Herald Tribune*, among others.
There are 3 Czech radio stations
and 2 TV channels. Satellite TV
from Germany and America is
available on pay televisions in
the large hotels.

Money Matters

The Czechoslovak unit of
currency is the crown (kčs). One
crown equals one hundred
hellers (h), though you will not
find many of the latter in modern
Prague.
It is still illegal to take Czech
money out of the country but
there are no restrictions on
importing or exporting hard

currency. It is virtually
impossible to change Czech
money for any Western
currencies. Even the banks treat
hard currency as a precious
commodity so take plenty.
Money may be changed at the
airport, in banks, major hotels,
Čedok offices and, nowadays, at
independent exchange offices in
the central areas. (Rates vary
little.) Every day without fail
someone or other will approach
you in the street and murmur
'tauschen,' or 'change'. These
black market money dealers
(some professional, some
amateur) should be ignored as
exchanging money in this way
still constitutes an offence. In any
case you will find that in these
days of rapid inflation the touts
rarely offer an attractive rate.
Credit cards are now accepted
in hotels, in the more expensive
restaurants and by Čedok.
Travellers cheques can be
changed at banks and exchange
offices and used for payment in
Tuzex shops. Private exchange
offices may offer more
advantageous rates in the near
future, as the Czech Central
Bank has devalued the crown.
The main bank, (**Státní banka
Československa**), is at Na
příkopě 28. *Open:* Monday-
Friday 08.00 to 17.00 hrs,
Saturday 08.30 to 13.00 hrs.
Outside the city centre, banks
open from 08.00 to noon *or*
14.00 hrs.

Opening Times

Banks

Monday to Friday 08.00 to 12.00
or 14.00 hrs (in the city centre:
08.00 to 17.00 hrs and Saturday
08.30 to 13.00 hrs).

DIRECTORY

Department stores
Monday to Friday 08.00 to 19.00 hrs, Saturday 08.00 to 16.00 hrs.

Food shops
Monday to Friday 08.00 to 18.00 hrs, Saturday 07.00 to 12.00 hrs.

Museums and galleries
Tuesday to Sunday 10.00 to 17.00 or 18.00 hrs (Jewish museum closed Saturday).

Offices
Monday to Friday 08.30 to 17.00 hrs.

Post Offices
Monday to Friday 08.00 to 19.00 hrs; Saturday 08.00 to 12.00 hrs; the Main Post Office in Jindřišská 14 is open 24 hours.

Personal Safety
Prague is still a comparatively safe city to walk in and ride around, though street crime is on the increase. As everywhere today, keep an eye on your bag or wallet in crowds, store valuables in the hotel safe and remember to lock you car.

Pharmacist (Lékárnat)
A 24-hour service can be found at:
Na příkopé 7, Praha 1 (tel: 22 00 81)
Ječná 1, Praha 2 (tel: 26 71 81)
Pod marjánkou 12, Břevnov, Praha 6 (tel: 35 09 67)
Obráncú míru 48, Praha 7 (tel: 37 83 80)
Moskevská 41, Praha 10 (tel: 72 44 76).

Places of Worship
The majority of Czech believers are Roman Catholic. Masses (in Czech) are held regularly on Sundays in most of the major Prague churches, for example St Vitus or St James, where some high masses are accompanied by music. Times of services vary, so check notice boards before you set out.
Protestant (Hussite) services are held at St Nicholas's Church in Old Town Square.
The medieval Old-New Synagogue in the Josefov district is still open for worship. Check with your hotel for details.

Police
The police are known as the *Veřejná Bezpečnost* (the letters VB can be seen on the sides of their white and yellow cars). The central police station is at Konviktská 14, Praha 1 (tel: 21 21 11 11).
In emergencies dial 158.
For registration and visa extensions go to the station at Olšanska 2, Praha 3. *Open:* Monday to Friday 08.00 to 12.00 hrs and 12.30 to 15.30 hrs; *Closed:* Wednesday pm.

Post Office
Post boxes, on the sides of buildings, are painted orange and blue. Most hotels sell stamps and have facilities for posting letters. **Postage stamps** can also be bought in shops selling stationery or postcards.
The central post office is at Jindřišská 14, Praha 1 (tel: 26 48 41 or 26 41 93). *Open:* 24 hours.
Poste Restante letters may be addressed here.
Telegrams can be sent from any post office and from most hotels. There is a **telex** service at main post offices and major hotels.
Post office opening times:
Monday to Friday 07.00 to 15.00

Perfect symmetry, with a T-shirt's aid

hrs (Wednesdays to 18.00 hrs);
Saturdays 08.00 to 12.00 hrs.

Public Holidays
1 January – New Year's Day
Easter Monday (moveable)
1 May – Labour Day
9 May – National Day
25–26 December – Christmas

Public Transport
Czechoslovakia operates a
cheap and efficient transport
system.

Buses
The main bus station is situated
at **Florenc** (Metro: Florenc).
Buses travel from here to Brno,
Bratislava, Karlovy Vary, Plzeň,
etc, but you may need a
reservation (tel: 22 14 45–9).

Trains
These are generally cheaper
than buses, providing you don't
travel on the express (*rýchlik*)
for which there is a surcharge.
Trains are operated by ČSD (the
Czechoslovak State Railways).
Tickets are generally valid for
one day but for long distance
journeys (over 125 miles
(200 km), buy a three-day ticket
which will allow you to break
your journey overnight if you
wish. First and second class
seats are available on all trains.
Sleepers and international rail
tickets are booked through
Čedok, *not* at stations, and the
fare is expected to be paid in
hard currency.
International trains leave from
Hlavní nádraží, Vítězného února,
Praha 2.
Other Prague stations:
Praha-Střed, Hybernská, Praha 1
(for most domestic services).
Praha-Smíchov, Nádražní, Praha
5 (for Karlštejn and Plzeň).

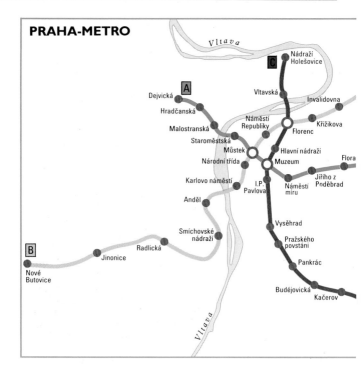

For train information: tel: 26 49 30 or 236 44 41.

Domestic Air Services
These operate between Prague and Bratislava, Piezšťany, Ostrava and Sliac. ČSA airline office: Revoluční 1, Praha 1 (tel: 21 4 6).

City Transport
Prague has an excellent transportation system, with buses, trams and a highly efficient metro. Tickets, valid for all three, are on sale at news-stands (PNS), tobacconists and at metro stations. One ticket is required per journey; if you change your mode of transport en route you will need a new ticket. 24-hour passes are available. There are no student reductions but children under 10 and senior citizens over 70 travel free.

For information – tel: 235 58 50. Routes and timetables for trams and buses are listed at stops. Buy a ticket before boarding and punch in the machine by the door. There are a restricted number of night services. (Night trams have blue numbers.)

The Metro
The metro is clean, fast and cheap and operates from 05.00 to 24.00 hrs. There are 3 lines:

Line A (green) from Dejvická to
Skalka.
Line B (orange) from Nové
Butovice to Českomoravská,
intersecting with C at Florenc
and with A at Můstek.
Line C (red) from Nádraží
Holešovice to Háje, intersecting
with A at Muzeum.
The letter M with an arrow
pointing downwards, marks the
entrance to a station. Buy your
ticket from the machine and you
can travel any distance with free
transfers between lines. There
are maps at all stations and clear
route direction signs. On each
train, a recorded voice
announces the next station.

Taxis
Taxis abound in Prague. With
the onset of private enterprise
many citizens have taken to
moonlighting as drivers, swelling
the ranks of the already prolific
state-controlled cabs. An

Underground life in Prague

DIRECTORY

unoccupied taxi has a lit-up sign and may be hailed in the street or hired from a taxi rank outside hotels, stations and the large department stores. All registered cabs should have a meter clearly displayed.
For radio cabs – tel: 20 29 51–5.

Senior Citizens

Apart from free travel for over-70s on the city transport, there are no special concessions or facilities for senior citizens. However, Saga, who organise holidays for senior citizens, do have trips to Prague. They can be contacted at: *UK*: Saga Holidays, Saga Building, Middelburg Square, Folkestone, Kent, CT20 1AZ (tel: (0303) 857000).

Even street scenes can be sublime

USA: Saga International, 120 Boylston Street, Boston, Mass. 02116 (tel: (617) 451–6808). Prague is very cheap, so senior citizens on a budget will find it an economical destination.

Student and Youth Travel

The **Youth Travel Agency (ČKM-SSM)** is at Žitná 12, Praha 2. There is also a **Juniorhotel** (for under 30s) at the same address – tel: 29 99 49. YHA members are entitled to discounts here and should contact this office to find out where other accommodation is available.
For International Student Identity Cards go to the ČKM-SSM office at Jindřišská 28, Praha 1 (tel: 26

85 07), taking a good supply of passport-size photographs. There are still very few instant photo booths in Czechoslovakia. Student cards entitle you to reductions on international trains, but not domestic transport. Many museums also offer a 50 per cent reduction for students. The **American Hospitality Centre** in Malé náměstí 14, Praha 1 (tel: 236 74 86), is a popular meeting place for young Western tourists. If you want to meet the locals, try going to discos at the Obecní dům (People's House), or queue up with young Czechs outside the discotheques of Wenceslas Square (see **Culture and Entertainment** p. 104). Ask Čedok how to find out about events at the Carolinum (Charles University). In the summer, try the open air swimming pools or parks; or in the winter, try a soccer or hockey match at one of the major sports stadia. (See **Sport and Leisure**.)

Telephones
Coin operated telephones can be found in all the usual places – on the street, at metro stations etc. Many boxes take only local calls. If you wish to make an international call, look out for the specially marked booths in the city centre and at the main post offices, eg Jindřišská 14, Praha 1. Enquiries – for Prague 120 for Czechoslovakia 121 for international calls 01 49. Booking international calls 01 35; booking trunk calls 102. Dialling codes for calls to Prague:
from Australia 0011–42 2
from Eire 16–42 2

from New Zealand 00 42 2
from the UK 010 42 2
from the US and Canada 001.
Dialing codes for calls from Prague:
to Australia 0061
to Eire 00 353
to New Zealand 00 64
to the UK 00144
to the US and Canada 001.
Dial area code omitting first 0 then subscriber's number.

Time
Czechoslovakia follows Central European Time, equivalent to Greenwich Mean Time + 1 hour
or
US Eastern Standard Time + 7 hours
From March to late September, clocks are put forward one hour (GMT +2 hours)
Time differences based on GMT:
Australia +7–9 hours
Canada $-4^{1}/_{2}$–10 hours
New Zealand +11 hours
US −6–12 hours

Tipping
Tipping is commonplace in Czechoslovakia. Hotel staff, tour guides, taxi drivers, waiters, cloakroom and lavatory attendants all expect tips. With current inflation rates, it is impossible to specify amounts, but small coins for cloakroom attendants and ten per cent of the bill in restaurants and taxis is a fair guide.

Toilets
Public toilets are not easy to find. The best bet is a metro station or hotel. Look out for the sign 'WC', but you may also see the Czech words *Muži* or *Páni* (men) and *Ženy* or *Dámy* (women).

DIRECTORY

Tourist Offices

Čedok, 17–18 Old Bond Street, London W1X 4RB (tel: (071) 629 6058).

Čedok, 10 East 40th Street, New York, NY 10016 (tel: (212) 689 9720).

There are numerous Čedok branches in Prague, specialising in various aspects of travel, theatre ticket allocation, etc. See the main office for details: Čedok, Na příkopě 18, Praha 1 (tel: 212 71 11, telex: 121109 or 121809). Čedok also run sightseeing tours of the city including a visit to 'U Fleku' brewery and cruises on the River Vltava. For more information on these and excursions to other Bohemian towns and historic castles, contact any Čedok office.

Travel Agencies

ČKM-SSM, Žitná 12, Praha 2 (tel: 29 99 49).

Autoturist, Opletalova 29, Praha 1 (tel: 22 48 28).

Balnea, Pařižská 11 (tel: 232 19 38) (Spa specialists).

Sport-Turist, Národní 33 (tel: 26 33 51).

Pragotour, U Obecního domu, Praha 23 (tel: 231 72 81).

What to take

Pack as for any other European destination. Do not forget an international adaptor for any electrical appliances.

Wheelchair Access

Prague makes few concessions to wheelchairs. The tower of the Old Town Hall has a lift and some of the entrances to Prague Castle have ramp access but the public transport system, most shops and many of the sights have steps only. Most of the new hotels do have some facilities for the disabled – check with the tourist office or travel agents.

Dignity with a dash of colour: the Civic Forum building with banner

LANGUAGE

Czech is a Slavonic language, closely related to Russian, Polish, Serbo-Croat and Bulgarian and spoken by more than 10 million people. A few minutes spent learning some simple words will enable you to wander round the city with greater freedom and ensure you a warmer welcome.

Useful Words and Phrases

		Pronounciation guide
hello/good day	dobrý den	*dobree den*
goodbye	na shledanou	*nah-skhleddunnow*
good evening	dobrý večer	*dobree vecher*
good night	dobrou noc	*dobrow nots*
please/you're welcome	prosím	*prosseem*
thank you	děkuji	*dyekoo-yi*
yes	ano	*unnoh*
no	ne	*neh*
excuse me	promiňte	*prohminte*
where?	kde	*gdeh*
when?	kdy	*gdy*
how much?	kolik	*kollick*
I	já	*yah*
we	my	*mee*
left	vlevo	*vlevoh*
right	vpravo	*vprahvoh*
straight on	hned	*ned*
near	blízko	*bleezkoh*
far	daleko	*dullekkoh*
I don't speak Czech	nemluvím česky	*nemlooveem cheski*
can you speak English?	mluvíte anglicky?	*mlooveete anglitski*
my name is	jmenuji se	*menooyi say*

Numbers

one	jeden(m) jedna(f) jedno(n)	*yedden, yednah, yednoh*
two	dva(m) devě(f)	*dvah, dvyeh*
three	tři	*tzhee*
four	čtyři	*shteezhee*
five	pět	*pyet*
six	šest	*shest*
seven	sedem	*seddum*
eight	osm	*ossum*
nine	devět	*devvyet*
ten	deset	*desset*

LANGUAGE

Days of the Week

English	Czech	Pronunciation
Sunday	neděle	*neddyelleh*
Monday	pondělí	*pondyelle*
Tuesday	úterý	*ooteree*
Wednesday	středa	*stzheddah*
Thursday	čtvrtek	*shtvertek*
Friday	pátek	*pahtek*
Saturday	sobota	*sobbottah*

Signs

entrance	vchod
exit	východ
emergency exit	nouzový východ
no entrance	vstup zakazán
toilet	záchod
gentleman	páni
ladies	dámy
men	muži
women	ženy
stop!	zastavte!
caution!	pozor!
no parking	parkování zakázáno
closed	zavěno
open	otevřeno
cash desk	pokladna
reserved, occupied	obsazený
vacant	volný
no smoking	kouření zakázáno
push	tam
pull	sem
restaurant	restaurace
post office	pošta
telephone	telefon
taxi	taxi
street	ulice
buffet	bufet
museum	muzeum
theatre	divadlo
cinema	kino/biograf
bookshop	knihkupectví
pharmacist	lékárna

INDEX

INDEX/ACKNOWLEDGEMENTS

The Automobile Association would like to thank the following photographers, libraries and associations for their assistance in the preparation of this book.

ANTONY SOUTER took all the photographs in this book (© AA Photo Library) except:

J ALLAN CASH PHOTOLIBRARY 80 Karlstejn Castle, 81 St Barbara's Cathedral, 88 Hikers, Low Tatra Mountains.

P ATTERBURY 9 Bridges and city, 18 Hotel Evropa, 23 View of city, 119 Window detail, 122 Detail of tower in city.

HULTON-DEUTSCH 14/15 Revolt at Prague, 20 Wrecked Russian tank.

INTERNATIONAL PHOTOBANK Cover St Nicholas's Church.

MARY EVANS PICTURE LIBRARY 13 Execution of Hus.

NATURE PHOTOGRAPHERS LTD 84 European lynx (E A Janes), 85 Lizard orchid (P R Sterry), 86 Wall lizard (S C Bisserott), 89 Penduline tit (P R Sterry), 90 Ural owl (D A Smith).

THE MANSELL COLLECTION LTD 10 Wenceslas.